You, Me and God

THE THREEFOLD CORD IS NOT EASILY BROKEN

Dr. Gene and Sue Lingerfelt

You, Me and God

THE THREEFOLD CORD IS NOT EASILY BROKEN

Dr. Gene and Sue Lingerfelt

Harrison House
Tulsa, Oklahoma

You, Me and God
A Threefold Cord Is Not Easily Broken
ISBN 1-57794-166-7
Copyright © 1998 by Dr. Gene & Sue Lingerfelt
P.O. Box 121234
Arlington, Texas 76012

Published by Harrison House, Inc.
P.O. Box 35035
Tulsa, Oklahoma 74153

Contents

Introduction   7

**Section 1   The Essential Ingredients
              for a Successful Marriage**   9

    Chapter 1   The Winning Results of Loving Yourself   11

    Chapter 2   Mastering the Power of Nurturing   29

Section 2   Becoming One Flesh   53

    Chapter 3   Exploring God's Wonderful Plan
                          for Your Marriage   55

    Chapter 4   Achieving Unity in Your Marriage   75

**Section 3   Solving the Mystery of
              Effective Communication**   89

    Chapter 5   The Power of Listening and Loving   91

    Chapter 6   Putting in What You Want to Get Out   109

Section 4   Loving for a Lifetime   117

    Chapter 7   How to Get All the Romance You Want!   119

    Chapter 8   Finding the Love That Will Never Fail   129

Introduction

And now abideth faith, hope, charity [love],
these three; but the greatest of these is
charity [love].

1 Corinthians 13:13

From the time we're children, we are taught and trained to believe that someday, when we grow up, we will fall in love. We're taught that this experience will be grand and glorious. It will be a wonderful romantic adventure.

Then all of a sudden, we're grown, we get married, and when we've traveled down the road of marriage a few years, we wake up one day and say to ourselves, "I don't feel like I used to feel about her," or "I don't feel like I used to feel about him."

It's an unsettling feeling in the very foundations of our souls. We don't understand how our intense emotions at the beginning of our marriage just aren't there anymore. We want help but don't know what to do in this heart-gripping situation.

Some well-meaning Christians will tell you, "Well, just stick it out. You know, that's the Christian thing to do. Just hang in there. Maybe it will work itself out and get better."

But no marriage will just "work itself out." It will only work itself into separation and alienation—either emotionally, physically or both.

Proverbs 21:21 NIV begins the unraveling of the answer: **He who pursues righteousness and love finds life, prosperity and honor.**

To find the romance again, to find a deeper connection to your spouse, you need to pursue love again. And no matter how you feel right now, you really can find it.

You, Me and God is a book full of practical tools based on God's Word to help you get back what may have diminished—even if it's just a little. Whether your marriage is good and doing OK, or on a fast track to divorce, this book will help you discover the positive potential your marriage has. There really is a constructive way for *all* marriages to succeed.

In chapter after chapter, we teach truths we've learned through almost two decades of teamwork, compromise and continuous companionship.

God loves you and wants you to partake of all the good things He created—including a wonderfully fulfilling marriage. What you will learn from this book is how to achieve what He originally created.

This book really is for every marriage, because every marriage can be better.

Dr. Gene and Sue Lingerfelt

SECTION 1

The Essential Ingredients for a Successful Marriage

Thou shalt love the Lord thy God with all thy heart, and with all thy soul, and with all thy strength, and with all thy mind; and thy neighbour as thyself.

Luke 10:27

CHAPTER 1

The Winning Results of Loving Yourself

Of all the endeavors you could ever attempt in life, achieving a successful marriage is definitely the most rewarding. You could work at becoming a corporate magnate, a powerful CEO or a chief surgeon. But none of these can even compare to the triumph of successfully attaining a relationship marked by unity, devoted companionship, unconditional love and true romance.

The reason no natural endeavor can compare is because a truly successful marriage comes from the supernatural, from the Source of all creation, from God Himself. Yes, it takes your effort and your cooperation, but God is the Source of all real success.

Nonetheless, just like all natural pursuits, the road of marriage is filled with opportunities to quit. But if you learn the secrets of how to stay in the game and win, the victory will be like no other you could ever experience.

It's a victory that you will savor, a victory that will draw you and your spouse into a oneness only God could create.

When you make the choice to work at your marriage and improve it—regardless of its present qualities—you enter into a level of deep personal satisfaction, a level of knowing that you did your best and fulfilled your dream...you achieved a marriage of heaven on earth.

Adam and Eve, the first man and woman to experience this holy union, were made as the supreme examples of God's creative power. They were created to rule, to become one flesh and to always be together.

But as most couples who have been married any length of time have discovered, to always be together takes work—teamwork.

For a marriage to be successful and mutually fulfilling, both persons in the relationship must apply the same skill and initiative to the marriage as they would to any other endeavor. For example, people will work vigorously and with dedication at their job or at their education. They'll even go to the gym faithfully and work out, but if they don't work at the most important thing God gave to them—their marriage—it is doomed to fail.

And, unfortunately, failed marriages are as common as weddings. The divorce rate in the United States is higher than in any other civilized nation. And sadly enough, the rate among Christians is only slightly lower than the national average where one out of every two marriages ends in divorce.

But in God's Word there are solutions. His Word is full of riches that will make your marriage successful and fulfilling.

Making Your Marriage a Success

Now, let's clarify that a successful marriage is not a perfect marriage. But it is a marriage that is growing. It's a marriage where there is a genuine partnership between the husband and wife, and where the relationship is continually growing to new levels of trust, love and companionship.

We have found that to gain and maintain a steady rate of growth in your marriage, three basic and critical ingredients are required. These three ingredients are essential for any of the other relationship principles we will teach you to work out, and they will make a difference in your marriage. So take these to heart as the foundation of your growing relationship.

The first critical ingredient you need is KNOWLEDGE ACTED UPON. If you gain knowledge, especially from the pages of this book, but don't act upon it, that knowledge will accomplish absolutely nothing in your life or your marriage.

The knowledge you need to make your marriage succeed is simply "how to act in marriage." No one should assume that they automatically know how to act in a marriage relationship. That's because most of us, and truthfully, probably all of us, learned some wrong things from the role models we saw around us as we were growing up. The family members, friends and neighbors who influenced us as we developed and matured didn't always act out the behavior God has outlined in His Word for marriage.

So if there is a problem in your marriage, it could be rooted in either you or your spouse (or both of you) not knowing how to act in married life, or in one of you refusing to act right in the relationship. Not acting properly in the marriage relationship is either a result of ignorance of how to act, which can be cured by knowledge, or stubbornness, which is cured by a change of heart. We'll give you solutions for both of these problems in later chapters.

Now, the second critical ingredient for a successful marriage is EFFORT. We mentioned this at the beginning of this chapter. Marriage is teamwork. You will have to put forth effort to make your marriage all that you desire and all that God created it to be. Putting forth effort means replacing your old behavior patterns with new behavior patterns. It means not giving up and taking the easy way out, or just coasting along. It means exercising the third critical ingredient, which is PERSEVERANCE.

Perseverance is acting the way you know you should even when your old self and your old habits try to reassert their influence in your daily life. If you allow them to, your old habits will become like a snowball rolling down a hill. They'll gain momentum more and more, and the results will grow bigger and bigger.

Well, the dynamic of perseverance is the same way. If you really want a better marriage, you'll persevere and the momentum will gain until you really do have an improved, successful marriage and a growing relationship.

Applying all three of these success ingredients to your own life before your marriage is what we call "getting your own act together." In order for you to properly relate to others, especially to your spouse, you will have to first get your own act together.

Learning to Love Yourself

One of the most important factors in getting your own act together so you can have a successful marriage is learning to love yourself. In order for you to love your husband or wife as you should, you really do have to love your own self. You have to have a good self-image.

Too many times in a marriage there is a downward cycle of two people, either because of their egos or insecurities, taking verbal shots at each other. Through their words and behavior, they constantly tear each other down, and by tearing each other down, they tear their marriage apart. It's literally impossible to have a happy, healthy marital relationship when one or both of the partners are suffering from a poor self-image.

But when both people have a healthy self-image, then they can freely and properly speak positive and uplifting words to one another. They can speak words of peace, encouragement, love and edification. Instead of tearing one another down, they'll be building each other up—and thus building up their marriage relationship.

In Ephesians 5:25-33, the apostle Paul wrote:

> **Husbands, love your wives, even as Christ also loved the church, and gave himself for it; that he might sanctify and cleanse it with the washing of water by**

Early on in our marriage, and even before we married, Gene began to work on my self-esteem. He recognized my weakness. Whether it was Valentine's Day or Sweetest Day, he often wouldn't send me flowers or candy. He'd give me a Bible. We laugh a lot about this now, but at the time I couldn't figure out why he did that. I thought he was trying to communicate to me that he wanted me to study and know the Bible, to be sure of the Word. Well, he did, but what he really was trying to do was get me to use the Word of God to build myself up and prepare me. He wanted me to find my self-image in the Word.

—Sue

the word, that he might present it to himself a glorious church, not having spot, or wrinkle, or any such thing; but that it should be holy and without blemish.

So ought men to love their wives as their own bodies. He that loveth his wife loveth himself. For no man ever yet hated his own flesh; but nourisheth and cherisheth it, even as the Lord the church: For we are members of his body, of his flesh, and of his bones.

For this cause shall a man leave his father and mother, and shall be joined unto his wife, and they two shall be one flesh. This is a great mystery: but I speak concerning Christ and the church.

Nevertheless let every one of you in particular so love his wife even as himself; and the wife see that she reverence her husband.

According to the Word, when you love yourself, whether you are the husband or the wife, you are then able to love others, including your spouse. Having positive self-esteem contributes to the success of your marriage. A successful marriage—and the result of two people with positive self-esteem—is a growing, dynamic relationship between two people, where the personalities of both partners continue to develop.

If you tear your partner down because you don't love yourself, then you need to work on developing a positive self-image. You need to practice reinforcing positive ways of viewing yourself. If you learn to see yourself in a positive way, then you won't try to build yourself up by tearing others down. It's so vital to learn this, and not tear down your marriage partner. Realize that your partner in life is someone very special. That person is someone God Himself has given to you.

Whether you realize it or not, loving other people and building them up is actually an extension of how you feel about yourself. If you have a positive attitude toward your own self, then you can be effective in reaching out to others and ministering to other people—including your mate.

In 1 John 4:7-8, the apostle John wrote, **Beloved, let us love one another: for love is of God; and every one that loveth is born of God, and knoweth God. He that loveth not knoweth not God; for God is love.**

Your capacity to love others is based upon your capacity to love yourself.

The degree to which you are able to love yourself is the degree to which you will be able to love others, so it really is critical to love yourself.

Keep in mind that self-love is not the same as selfishness because it does not involve one's ego. Don't confuse the

After Gene and I married, he always encouraged me. I was very shy as a child growing up, and as a young adult. I certainly never wanted to speak publicly in front of people. But he would tell me I could do anything. He told me I was talented and had something important to say. He believed that, and because he believed it, and because I knew he knew me best, I believed it.

But it could have been just the opposite. He could have said, "You're a dumb cluck. You don't know anything. Where did you get your Bible knowledge? The thrift store?"

That would not have built me up, nor prepared me for the ministry to which God called us.

So often we wonder why our spouse isn't progressing, isn't able to help us, doesn't want to go out and get involved in church or other things...a lot of times it's because they feel inadequate and need someone to build them up. The best someone is you.

—Sue

two. Selfishness and self-love are opposites. They are worlds apart. When a person has a healthy self-esteem, he or she does not put their own needs ahead of another person. They are simply confident of who they are.

A husband or wife who is self-confident is not threatened by the presence of success in the life of his or her mate. They are not threatened by the happiness of their spouse—and they aren't afraid to contribute to their spouse's individual success.

Contributing to the success of your marriage partner doesn't take away from your own self-worth or from who you are as an individual. It doesn't mean you aren't worth as much as he or she is. Actually, contributing to the success of another increases your value. Jesus said in Luke 6:38, **Give, and it shall be given unto you; good measure, pressed down, and shaken together, and running over, shall men give into your bosom. For with the same measure that ye mete withal it shall be measured to you again.**

If you give into the life of your partner and are a blessing to them, that doesn't denigrate your life at all. It builds you up, as well as your marriage.

Avoiding the Extremes

In the practice of self-love, there are two perversions of this truth that can be taken to extremes, and we need to guard ourselves against those. The first is something we mentioned before, ego involvement, and the second is a self-critical attitude.

The ego-involved person judges outward circumstances based on their emotions and how it affects them. In doing this, they judge every circumstance, idea, suggestion and opinion only by what they think or only upon their own personal experiences. This is the kind of person who hears only half of an idea and quickly condemns it, saying, "Well, that sure is a stupid idea."

An ego-involved person specializes in belittling and pulling down his or her partner in order to bring that partner down to his own level, in order to make him or herself feel greater and more important. Obviously, this does not enhance the marriage, nor does it lead to romance.

The other perversion is a self-critical attitude. The self-critical person judges him or herself emotionally by what's going on around him. This is the kind of person who says, "Oh, how could I be that stupid?" just because the smallest thing went wrong in his or her present circumstances.

Most people are guilty of speaking in these two ways at one time or another, but the problem is serious if they live habitually in one of these extremes.

Both of these extremes are rooted in a poor self-image. Self-depreciation, or self-criticism, is a sign of a negative self-image. The person who is always putting himself down doesn't feel good about himself.

Likewise, the person who is always putting others down also has a negative self-image. He truthfully hates himself. In other words, if a person really felt good about himself and knew who he was in Christ Jesus, then he wouldn't need to say things to make others feel bad about who they are.

For example, a man who is physically abusive towards his wife has two things operating in his life. First, he may not know how to act, or he may be stubborn and just want to do his own thing. And second, he doesn't like himself. If he felt positive about who he is, he would not have a need to beat up anyone, let alone his partner in life.

To have a positive self-image or high self-esteem is to have a healthy perspective of yourself. It's knowing who you are in Christ Jesus. As a believer, you have been made in the image of God. Genesis 1:27 says, **So God created man in his own image, in the image of God created he him; male and female created he them.** Although every human being is unique, everyone is made in the image and likeness of God. That in itself ought to be reason enough to treat yourself, as well as others, with love, honor and respect.

As a believer, you also have been made new. Second Corinthians 5:17 says, **Therefore if any man be in Christ, he is a new creature: old things are passed away; behold, all things are become new.**

Whatever you once were like, when you were born again, you became brand new. You got a fresh start. But if you only changed on the inside and not the outside, you can start today to make some outward changes. You have the life of God on the inside of you, the very essence and power of Almighty God Himself. He placed His Spirit within you when you were born again. You have great value and worth. Your life is very important and everything you do every day is very important to God. Who you are and what you are matters to Him. When that is a revelation to you, it will matter to you too. Then you'll have a healthy self-image.

First Corinthians 3:16-17 says, **Know ye not that ye are the temple of God, and that the Spirit of God dwelleth in you? If any man defile the temple of God, him shall God destroy; for the temple of God is holy, which temple ye are.**

God has called you holy. That's powerful. That's healthy! If you'll search the scriptures for all of the verses containing the phrases "in Him" and "in Christ," you will find out who you really are...and your confidence will soar.

Having a healthy self-image is neither arrogance nor conceit. It's simply having a healthy respect for yourself. It's being careful not to underrate yourself. It's believing you are who God has said you are in His Word. It's seeing yourself the way God sees you. When you have a healthy self-esteem, you accept yourself as a worthwhile person. You dismiss doubts about your ability to have successful relationships with others, particularly your partner. You are enabled and empowered to direct your energy toward understanding and helping your partner.

It's so important to be realistic with yourself about your own self-image. You need to ask yourself questions to evaluate and examine how you're doing. Answer the following questions to determine areas in which you need to improve:

- What is my overall mental picture of myself?
- How do I view myself physically?
- How do I view myself mentally?
- How do I view myself emotionally?
- How do I view myself spiritually?
- How do I view myself socially?
- How do I view myself in my vocation?

It's good to be aware of whether or not you see yourself as kind, generous, emotionally stable, physically acceptable and good at your job, because the truth is, if you see yourself as fat, then fat you shall be. If you see yourself as incompetent, then incompetent you shall be. Proverbs 23:7 says that as a man thinks in his heart, so is he.

So even though it's good to know how you see yourself now, it's more beneficial to learn how God sees you. You have to renew your mind—to change the way you think. Romans 12:2 says, **And be not conformed to this world: but be ye transformed by the renewing of your mind, that ye may prove what is that good, and acceptable, and perfect, will of God.** You have to learn to think of yourself as God does.

And as you learn to see who you are in Christ, and as you develop your self-image from what God has said about you, you can be at peace that you are moving in the right direction. You have to walk by faith that you are improving and rest in that.

Hebrews 11:1 says, **Now faith is the substance of things hoped for, the evidence of things not seen.** Based on this scripture, when you hope for something and release your faith for it, it comes to pass. If you cannot see it with the eye of faith in your spirit, then it is unlikely that you will have it.

When someone wants to succeed at something, he envisions the successful outcome of that endeavor. When a professional football player, such as Dallas Cowboys quarterback Troy Aikman, is ready to throw the ball, he doesn't envision it being intercepted. He doesn't see a dropped pass. No, he's envisioning what he wants to come to pass. Sales people do the same thing. They use the positive power of their imaginations to help them succeed.

You and I are no different. We can preplay in our minds what we want to happen in our lives and, by releasing our God-given faith, watch it come to pass.

In the same way, if we see ourselves with negative qualities, then those negative qualities are what we will have.

Because of how we've often been raised and influenced by the church, regardless of denomination, we've often been exposed to the practice of being self-critical to ensure humility. To many people this is the righteous way to behave and speak. It sounds humble to them to tear themselves down or beat themselves up emotionally. But there is no biblical basis for being unnecessarily self-critical. Remember, you are made in the image of God. Who are you to be critical of God's creation?

King David said so eloquently in Psalm 139:13-16 NIV:

For you created my inmost being; you knit me together in my mother's womb. I praise you because I am fearfully and wonderfully made; your works

When I graduated from seminary, and Sue and I were interviewing for church positions, the interviewer would often ask, "Do you play the piano?"

"No," I'd reply.

"Does your wife?"

"No."

"Does she sing?"

"No."

I had a higher vision than just having a helpmate in the ministry who could play the piano or sing. I wanted one who could stand up and minister the Word and be a blessing to people. But Sue lacked self-confidence. So I sought to build her up.

Self-confidence is one of the major roadblocks to peace of mind. That's why people are tormented in their minds. They don't know who they are. They don't know where they're headed or what their destiny is.

King David said, All the days ordained for me were written in your book before one of them came to be (Psalm 139:16 NIV). If you don't know the One Who's got the book, then you don't know your destiny and your purpose in life. Self-confidence is your belief in your own ability to come to grips with problems and solve them with God's help. Self-confidence equips you emotionally to meet the challenges of life with equanimity and determination.

—Gene

are wonderful, I know that full well. My frame was not hidden from you when I was made in the secret place. When I was woven together in the depths of the earth, your eyes saw my unformed body. All the days ordained for me were written in your book before one of them came to be.

That is who you are. Never criticize such a beautiful creation.

Loving Your Closest Neighbor

Jesus told the Pharisees the greatest commandment of all in Matthew 22:34-39:

> But when the Pharisees had heard that he had put the Sadducees to silence, they were gathered together. Then one of them, which was a lawyer, asked him a question, tempting him, and saying, Master, which is the great commandment in the law? Jesus said unto him, Thou shalt love the Lord thy God with all thy heart, and with all thy soul, and with all thy mind. This is the first and great commandment. And the second is like unto it, Thou shalt love thy neighbour as thyself.

When you begin to love yourself and know who you are in Christ Jesus, you begin to walk in a healthy self-image. Only then can you truly begin to love your neighbor as yourself.

So who is your closest neighbor?

The one you live with. The one God has made your partner in life.

There are people—and you may know one or be one—who will witness on the streets, who will visit the detention center, who will minister at the jail or visit the hospital, but they don't know how to love their closest neighbor. They will reach out to strangers before they'll meet the needs of their own husband or wife. Because they have a poor self-image, or they're insecure, they hold their marriage and their entire family back. They simply don't love themselves. They don't have a healthy self-esteem that comes from knowing who they are in Christ.

If they could grasp this and dig into God's Word and discover who they are in Him, they would have a healthy recognition and honor for the natural endowments they possess—and that their spouse possesses. They also would reap the three greatest benefits of a healthy self-image: security, self-confidence and determination.

Security is the opposite of ego involvement, something we've already discussed. A secure person is open and honest. They have no need to speak in riddles. They have no need to exaggerate or brag. They are people filled with genuine and infectious enthusiasm. They are devoid of a critical spirit or attitude. They are not cynical or suspicious. They simply have no need to tear others down in order to build themselves up.

When a husband or wife is secure, they are not threatened when their spouse gets a new and better paying job. They don't react with criticism, but with rejoicing. They see that new job as a blessing to them as well, not as a burden or negative event.

Being secure leads to being self-confident. Now, self-confidence is really confidence in God on the inside of you, in what He has said in His Word about who you are in Him. Hebrews 10:35 tells us the value of this kind of confidence: **Cast not** away therefore your confidence, which hath great recompence of reward. Confidence has rewards—rewards of success.

Self-confidence is boldness. As a believer, God has placed His boldness on the inside of you. You are a new creature, remember? You have His nature and His characteristics on the inside of you. You are the righteousness of God in Christ. Proverbs 28:1 says, **The wicked flee when no man pursueth: but the righteous are bold as a lion.** To be bold as a lion, you have to have self-confidence!

Some people have a hard time with intimacy. In order to overcome that, they need self-confidence. Self-confidence precedes intimacy. If you are a person who is painfully shy, then you cannot develop close friends or the kind of relationship you need with your closest neighbor.

If you feel insecure and lack self-confidence, then you will be the type of person who wants the lights out and the covers pulled up to your nose...rather than being open and intimate with your spouse. But when you feel good about yourself, you can be more understanding and appreciative of your mate... not threatened. You can also more easily let your spouse know how worthwhile they are. And that will promote the closeness and love you are desiring in your marriage.

The third benefit of healthy self-esteem is **determination.** Determination is simply believing in yourself enough not to give up. It's making a definite decision to use the best of your abilities and the endowments God gave to you. A determined person doesn't give up on themselves or others—including their closest neighbor.

If you are determined to succeed in your marriage, then it is literally impossible for you to fail. To give up on anything is to admit defeat. Remember: quitters never win, and winners never quit.

If you've come to the place of resolve that your marriage will succeed, you've already won half the battle. If you choose to love yourself, you're even farther along on the road to victory, and closer than ever to loving your closest neighbor. You're definitely headed toward winning results, and you're closer than ever before to getting your own act together—the most important step in having a truly successful marriage.

CHAPTER 2

Mastering the Power of Nurturing

Learning to love yourself opens up the door to being able to truly love your closest neighbor. And loving your neighbor means reaching out to them and meeting their deepest needs–needs that God ordained no one else to meet except you, their precious husband or wife. Likewise, He predestined him or her to meet your needs as well, because marriage is a commitment to mutual need fulfillment.

Mutual need fulfillment is a mouthful that simply means if you want a marriage that is fulfilling to both you and your spouse, there are some steps you'll have to take to ensure it happens. It won't happen automatically. And you have to begin by learning what your spouse needs. After all, if you don't know your spouse's needs, how will you meet them?

"But, Gene and Sue, I'm the one who's not having my needs met!"

Hold on, we're going to show you how you can have your needs met in marriage...but part of the key to receiving is giving.

Whether you are the husband or the wife, when you married, you made a commitment to meet your spouse's needs. We often tell single men and women not to marry if they are not interested in meeting anyone else's needs, because mutual need fulfillment is part of what the marriage covenant was created to do.

God even recorded the concept of mutual need fulfillment in His Word with regard to our sexuality in marriage. It is important to Him, and He wants it to be important to us. First Corinthians 7:3-5 NIV says:

> **The husband should fulfill his marital duty to his wife, and likewise the wife to her husband. The wife's body does not belong to her alone but also to her husband. In the same way, the husband's body does not belong to him alone but also to his wife. Do not deprive each other except by mutual consent and for a time, so that you may devote yourselves to prayer. Then come together again so that Satan will not tempt you because of your lack of self-control.**

So it is very clear in God's Word that, regardless of what is politically correct in any society or culture, when you married, whether you are the husband or the wife, you gave up a part of yourself, of your life, and you gave up a part of your rights.

It's also clear that sex is not to be used as a weapon in marriage. We aren't to withhold ourselves from one another as punishment or as a way to express anger or disagreement. No, you need to verbally communicate and work out your disagreements–which we'll discuss in a later chapter–and never withhold sexually from one another, except as the Scripture says, for prayer and with mutual consent.

This concept of mutual need fulfillment is really the reason you married in the first place–whether you realize it or not. That's because there were obviously some needs in your life that you perceived your spouse could meet, and he or she obviously perceived the same about you. To deny this is simply to deny the truth. That's why people get married. They not only want each other, they need each other.

There are needs in your life that only your spouse can meet, and there are needs in his or her life that only you can meet. These needs are in every area of your lives. They are in the physical area, the emotional area, the mental area and the spiritual area. This is because you aren't married in just one area of your life.

Marriage doesn't affect just a part of you. No, it affects all of you. It affects every area of your life. That's why it is so important to minister to one another in every area. And ministering to our spouses is what this chapter is all about... to minister to your spouse's needs, you have to know their needs–specifically.

For example, a lot of times we think we are sensitive to the needs of others, when we really aren't. We think we are meeting the needs of our spouse, when in reality, we are living far from that place of ministry.

The root to this can often be in our own perceptions of what we believe meeting someone else's needs really involves. What we have to do to succeed is give up the role models we saw growing up, or the image in our minds as to what role we are supposed to be living in the marriage relationship, and instead, really tune in to our own husband or wife.

The Power of Nurturing

The power you have to transform your marriage is beyond what you have ever thought up to this point–and that power is so easy to attain. It's called nurturing. If you learn how to nurture your marriage relationship, specifically how to meet your spouse's needs, you literally can transform your married life into a growing and loving experience. By meeting one another's needs, you can create and maintain an actively loving environment that you live in all the time. You can even make it fun. When you learn the power of nurturing your marriage by making a daily conscientious effort to meet the needs of your mate, you will live in married love all the time!

The key to nurturing is knowing what your spouse's needs really are–not what you think their needs ought to be. You see, most marital journeys begin with high romantic intensity. As couples approach marriage, they honestly and usually have only a superficial awareness of each other's wants, needs and expectations. At this stage in marriage, it really doesn't matter though, because they seem to automatically meet one another's needs because they're on this romantic high, so to speak.

That's the way romance begins...but in time, it changes. As time goes on, more and more demands are often made on each of the partners, usually from the outside. So what began as complete focus and devotion to the girlfriend or boyfriend, now has to be shared with the demands of a job.

Later on, a baby is often added as a demand. And the list can go on and be as individually unique as the people are.

The effect of this natural order is that as outside demands increase, and more and more attention is given to those outside demands, the attention level given inside the marriage too often begins to diminish...and this is when the marriage ceases to be spontaneous. You've probably heard of the concept of marriage killing romance. This is what that concept refers to. But truthfully, it's not that marriage kills romance, it's just that people get back to the business of life, of going back to work–mentally and physically.

The Solution to Killed Romance

If your marriage fits this description, or you've gone through seasons of dying embers in the fire, there's a sure way to reignite the romance in your heart and spark a flame. In fact, we've already told you the secret: mutual needs fulfillment.

The matter of unfulfilled needs as a source of conflict can be avoided by the mutual meeting of one another's needs. In a successful marriage, each person is sensitive to, and attempts to meet, the needs of the other. Whether these needs are expressed or unexpressed, they are needs that need to be addressed. The following are three practical steps you can purposefully consider as you start becoming aware of what your spouse REALLY needs and how you can success-fully meet those needs. If you do, most likely, you'll reap the same kind of treatment if you do it with a whole heart in love and not give up your hope and your faith.

Awareness

Awareness is very important. You can't meet your spouse's needs if you are not aware of those needs. So you need to ask your husband or wife exactly what he or she wants. Now this may be awkward if you aren't normally this vulnerable with one another. But you've got to do it. You can't go by what you think your partner's needs are. It's really elementary: If you're a guy, you've never been a woman, so you honestly can't conceive what is important to a woman. And if you're a woman, you can't really know what a man deems as a need. So you have to be vulnerable, honest and loving. You have to ask, "What do you expect out of me?" and be willing and open to receive the answer wholeheartedly.

It is totally unreasonable and wrong to have an expectation, then to keep it a secret, but think you have the right to become angry when that expectation goes unfulfilled. You have to speak. You have to communicate.

We often talk to couples where one or both of the partners are angry because they aren't getting what they expect out of their husband or wife. But, they aren't letting the other one know exactly what it is they do expect!

There's no way to win in that situation. Your goal is to win in marriage, to have a wonderful, mutually fulfilling life of married love...and you can't do that if you don't really know what it is your spouse needs.

You see, marriage is a process...not a ceremony in front of a preacher on a given day in history. It's a process of a relationship evolving into what God called and ordained it to be. It's a process of getting to know one another, and enjoying the meeting of each other's needs because of your commitment of love, and your commitment to the marriage relationship.

Commitment

The second step to satisfying your spouse is commitment. That means it is your responsibility to get your needs met. If you won't let your husband or wife know your needs, by honestly and politely communicating them, you have no right to expect those needs to be met.

In other words, if you are mad because you aren't getting your needs met, it could be your own fault. Have you lovingly told your mate what you need? Are you equally desirous of meeting his or her needs as you are about having your own met?

If you are committed to meeting your spouse's needs and having your own needs met, you have to start by letting your partner know what your own are, and each of you has to be equally determined to meet those needs.

Action

If you are reading this book alone, and you're the one who's frustrated in the marriage, you're going to have to be the one to take action. Taking action means going out of your way, taking the first step and going the extra mile. If you're reading this book together, then you can take the first step together.

The first step is asking your spouse what his or her needs are and then acting to meet those needs on a daily basis. Whether you start out doing this alone or together, the results will be worth it. God can make your marriage all you've dreamed it to be. All He needs is your cooperation in applying His principles of walking in love and giving unconditional love and acceptance.

He is a loving God, and He wants the best for your married life. Remember, He created marriage and the family...and He created His plans to succeed. So, don't give up. Jeremiah 29:11 NIV says, **"For I know the plans I have for you," declares the LORD, "plans to prosper you and not to harm you, plans to give you hope and a future."**

Your marriage—regardless of whether it's good, needs a little help or a lot of help—is something God wants to succeed, and He will help you as long as you open the door for Him to work. We have a lot more ground to cover in this book, but these practical principles we're presenting are based on God's Word and His teachings regarding relationships and walking in love. Remember, He is on your side. He wants you to win in every area of life, including your marriage!

Getting Started

We've identified nine basic human needs that are common to all men and women to help you get started meeting the needs of your spouse. Now, there are far more than nine, but these will help you begin thinking in the right direction. As you read through these, be honest with yourself and ask yourself if you are already meeting that need in your spouse. If you aren't, then that's a great area in which to begin working.

The first basic human need is genuine love. All people, every man and woman, have a need for genuine love. Everyone wants to know there is someone in this world who truly loves them. We all want someone who loves us, not for what they can get from us, and not for what we are able to do, but because they simply do. We all need that unconditional, unique kind of love. As men and women, we also have unique ways of needing love expressed.

For example, men in particular have a need to feel *acceptance, admiration* and *appreciation.* It is important for wives to show their husbands that they accept them, admire them and appreciate them. If wives will do that, then their husbands will feel that genuine love they need.

Women, on the other hand, typically like to be shown they are *loved.* They like to be told that they are loved, and they want to hear why they are loved. And the interesting thing about women is that they want and need this attention often. We've teased between us that Sue wants to hear it every twenty-four hours—and that's absolutely true! It sounds a little more complicated than meeting a man's needs, but it really is the way to meet a woman's need for genuine love.

Women have a need to hear their husband recite, so to speak, all of their character traits that cause their husband to love them. They need to know they are cherished by their husbands. What the underlying truth is concerning this need to hear details of your devotion is that a woman wants to know she is meeting a need in your life that no other woman on earth could possibly ever meet. That's the bottom line.

So we highly encourage every husband to regularly recite to his wife all that she does for him that no other woman could ever do and do right!

The second basic human need we all have is security. We all want to feel secure emotionally, spiritually, financially and vocationally. To illustrate this, think of what happens to people, even people not directly affected, when they hear of

> *Men, brag on your wife. So many times there will be guys at a church event or somewhere else and they'll be bragging about how good my wife looks. And every time I look over at their wife, she's hanging her head, just waiting...she's been waiting for weeks for a compliment from this guy, and all he knows how to do is compliment other women! That's got to change. Men, if you're going to brag on a woman, brag on your own wife—and no one else's! Brag on your own wife and watch her come alive!*
>
> *—Gene*

a big layoff that some corporation is going to issue. It's both interesting and amazing how it reverberates through the psyche of American culture. The reason for this is the basic need we all have to be secure. We have a need to know that "all is well" and stable.

In the marriage relationship, women especially have a need for financial security. In our counseling and teaching, we have found that it often bothers a woman when her husband doesn't have life insurance, or when her husband doesn't want to get health insurance—for himself or the family. Women often don't like living in apartments or leasing for long periods of time. They need and want a home of their own. Why is this? Because they have a need to feel secure.

They don't want to weed someone else's yard, namely the landlord's. No, they want to have their own rose garden out front, and landscape according to their own ideas of where the shrubs should go.

These may seem insignificant to a man's way of thinking, but to a woman, they mean everything—namely something as big and important as security. Overall, no matter what the circumstances, women want to feel secure in the marriage.

Now, we've seen many men use the "D" word (divorce) to whip their wives into subjection, to make her do what he wants her to do. This is completely contrary to the Scriptures. In the book of Genesis, when God made man and woman He made them equal, male and female. God gave woman to man to be a helpmate—that's the word the Bible uses. And a helpmate is someone who comes alongside and helps.

God never gave woman to man for man to lord over her, to dominate her or to control her. The woman was a gift to him. Proverbs 18:22 says **Whoso findeth a wife findeth a good thing, and obtaineth favour of the LORD.** When a man finds a woman, he has found a blessing from God, and he should treat her as such.

When a man is domineering, he is selfish. He does damage to his own marriage that can take a long time to repair. Ephesians 5:18-21 admonishes us how we are to treat each other, build one another up and submit to one another:

> **And be not drunk with wine, wherein is excess; but be filled with the Spirit; speaking to yourselves in psalms and hymns and spiritual songs, singing and making melody in your heart to the Lord; giving thanks always for all things unto God and the Father in the name of our Lord Jesus Christ; submitting yourselves one to another in the fear of God.**

Now, even though God made man and woman equal, He *did* make the man the leader of the home. This means he's responsible for the condition of his home—physically, financially and spiritually. Therefore, men need wives who look to them as the leader of the home. Women need to allow their husbands to lead spiritually, and they can do this by allowing him to be the leader in all other ways.

Allowing him to lead in all the other areas creates a desire in a husband to lead his family spiritually. It doesn't matter if he isn't "as spiritual as you." If you submit to his leadership, God will meet him at his level. And if you refrain from trying to nudge him in this direction or that direction, you'll free up his ability to hear the voice of the Holy Spirit.

First Peter 3:1-6 refers to this wonderful way of encouraging your husband to be a leader and letting him know of your confidence in his leadership:

> Likewise, ye wives, be in subjection to your own husbands; that, if any obey not the word, they also may without the word be won by the conversation of the wives; while they behold your chaste conversation coupled with fear. Whose adorning let it not be that outward adorning of plaiting the hair, and of wearing of gold, or of putting on of apparel; but let it be the hidden man of the heart, in that which is not corruptible, even the ornament of a meek and quiet spirit, which is in the sight of God of great price.
>
> For after this manner in the old time the holy women also, who trusted in God, adorned themselves, being in subjection unto their own husbands: Even as Sara obeyed Abraham, calling him lord: whose daughters ye are, as long as ye do well, and are not afraid with any amazement.

Peter goes on with wonderful instruction for how husbands can love their wives and increase their wive's senses of true security:

> Likewise, ye husbands, dwell with them according to knowledge, giving honour unto the wife, as unto

the weaker vessel, and as being heirs together of the grace of life; that your prayers be not hindered.

Finally, be ye all of one mind, having compassion one of another, love as brethren, be pitiful, be courteous: Not rendering evil for evil, or railing for railing: but contrariwise blessing; knowing that ye are thereunto called, that ye should inherit a blessing.

For he that will love life, and see good days, let him refrain his tongue from evil, and his lips that they speak no guile: Let him eschew evil, and do good; let him seek peace, and ensue it. For the eyes of the Lord are over the righteous, and his ears are open unto their prayers: but the face of the Lord is against them that do evil.

1 Peter 3:7-12

The third basic human need is spiritual harmony. Both husbands and wives have an inner basic need to be in true spiritual harmony. This is especially true for Christian marriages. And it is far more than simply doctrinal agreement. This goes beyond the intellect and is a true oneness in seeking God. It is essential to have this element if you want to achieve the ultimate closeness that every couple desires.

The root to this need is that a man wants a wife who can lovingly appeal to him. That means to come to him and kindly discuss her concerns with a decision or an issue in the home. And a wife wants a husband who will include her in the decision-making process. By eliminating her from the decision making, he is lording over her and not treating her as the equal God created her to be. To involve your wife in the decision-making process is more than having her help make the list of the pros and cons. It's sitting down with her and going before our heavenly Father together in prayer.

And a man who truly wants to lead his home won't be intimidated by praying with his wife and children. Women need to see this. They need to see their husbands willing and wanting to pray with them and with their children. So often, it seems the number one complaint we hear of in homes is that a husband won't pray. Oh, he will at church if he's asked, but he's not willing to be vulnerable to his family. He sees this as weakness, when in reality, it proclaims from the rooftops strength to his wife and children.

Women need this strength in their homes. It lets them know there is a covering and protector in the home. It tells them there is someone interested in their spiritual welfare, and that of their children. It tells them that everything will be OK, that all is well, that all is secure.

The fourth basic human need is respect. Both husbands and wives have a need to be respected, to feel they are loved for who they are. Respect is demonstrated by never discrediting the other person, or demeaning them, either publicly or privately. Ephesians 5:22-33 NASB clearly speaks of this critical ingredient in marriage:

> **Wives, be subject to your own husbands, as to the Lord. For the husband is the head of the wife, as Christ also is the head of the church, He Himself being the Savior of the body.**

> **But as the church is subject to Christ, so also the wives ought to be to their husbands in everything.**

> **Husbands, love your wives, just as Christ also loved the church and gave Himself up for her; that He might sanctify her, having cleansed her by the washing of water with the word, that He might present to Himself the church in all her glory, having**

no spot or wrinkle or any such thing; but that she should be holy and blameless.

So husbands ought also to love their own wives as their own bodies. He who loves his own wife loves himself; for no one ever hated his own flesh, but nourishes and cherishes it, just as Christ also does the church, because we are members of His body.

For this cause a man shall leave his father and mother, and shall cleave to his wife; and the two shall become one flesh. This mystery is great; but I am speaking with reference to Christ and the church.

Nevertheless let each individual among you also love his own wife even as himself; and let the wife see to it that she respect her husband.

The vital element of mutual respect is critical to a successful marriage. If you don't value one another as equally important, your marriage will be full of hurt and potential destruction. Remember, God created us male and female. Both were created in the image of God. One is not more like God than the other. Consequently, one is not more important than the other. Men are sons of God, but women are daughters of God. God loves women the same as He loves men.

Therefore, God is not going to treat men and women differently. All of His ways as outlined in the Word of God are equally effective for men and women. This is important to understand and receive in your spirit, because your thinking affects your behavior.

If you realize that your spouse is made by God and is a son or daughter of God, then you are more apt to address them, whether publicly or privately or in front of the children, with utmost respect. Husbands and wives simply should never speak to one another disrespectfully in private, in front of anyone else and especially not in front of their children.

It's so very important to realize that, for example, if a woman speaks disrespectfully to her husband, especially in front of their children, she literally causes them to disrespect their father. And the odds are, the husband will never forgive her for that.

Likewise, men should avoid doing the same. Fathers really can't afford for their children to disrespect their wives, because of the powerful influence a mother has on her children. And more times than not, she is the one who spends the most amount of time with the children.

Children should never be allowed to speak disrespectfully to either of their parents. The way we handle this in our marriage is that if one of our children speaks inappropriately to their mother, and their father hears it, he does the correcting. If they speak that way to their father, then their mother does the correcting.

This accomplishes a twofold purpose. Number one, they know loudly and clearly that their father is on their mother's side. And number two, they realize quickly they are not the boss in the house and that they need to be respectful.

This is a powerful and effective tool in our home. It tells our children that we have a united front, that we are a team. As a result, our children know there is unity. If we let down our guard, then division will try to creep in, so we are diligent about our spiritual harmony.

The fifth basic human need we've identified is expressed gratitude. It's so easy in a marriage to get comfortable, forget about the other person and take one another for granted. Ingratitude is really one of the ugliest traits there is.

Unfortunately, this is one that husbands get caught up in all too often. It's so easy for men to take their wives' labor for granted, especially if their wife works in the home.

So often men get all caught up in work and the problems at work, that when they come home at night, they have their minds on their problems. They don't have their minds on how nice the house looks, or what a nice dinner is set before them, or how the children are doing in school. They need to slow down, get their priorities straight and express gratitude.

Women can get caught up in this as well. Whether the home is a dual-income family or not, women can forget to show appreciation and gratitude for the fact that their husband is working, providing finances, the home, the vacations, the clothing and all other necessities. The important thing isn't who contributes the most, but to show gratitude to each other for what each contributes to the marriage, to the home life and to each other.

The sixth basic human need we've identified, we believe is unique and usually not typically found in books on marriage. **It's the need to be attractive to others and also to be associated with attractive people.** Now, this particular basic human need has nothing to do with the images on the front of *People* magazine or *Glamour.* When we all dated and married, we knew age and gravity would have their effect eventually. No, that's not it at all. What we're identifying in this basic need is the radiance of your countenance. Your countenance is directly related to your outward maintenance. How you take care of yourself reflects what's on the inside of you. First Peter 3:1-6 NIV reveals where our beauty should lie and how it should reflect on our countenance:

> Wives, in the same way be submissive to your husbands so that, if any of them do not believe the word, they may be won over without words by the behavior of their wives, when they see the purity and reverence of your lives. Your beauty should not come from outward adornment, such as braided hair and the wearing of gold jewelry and fine clothes.
>
> Instead, it should be that of your inner self, the unfading beauty of a gentle and quiet spirit, which is of great worth in God's sight. For this is the way the holy women of the past who put their hope in God used to make themselves beautiful. They were submissive to their own husbands, like Sarah, who obeyed Abraham and called him her master. You are her daughters if you do what is right and do not give way to fear.

Now, in this passage, Peter was addressing the women of that time, but the principles are true for both men and women today. The point Peter made was for us to not be consumed with trying to be somebody else...trying to be attractive from the outside only, and not from the inside out. What he was encouraging us to do was to look as good as we can with what we've got.

For example, women like their husbands to shower and shave on a daily basis...and especially before getting close to them—including Saturdays, guys! They like for their husbands to wear shirts at the dinner table. When their husbands take them out for dinner, a quick drive through McDonald's is not what they have in mind.

And ladies...a woman needs and wants her man to express his desire for her. But if she looks exactly the same when he arrives home as she did when he left that morning, it could be a challenge for him to be attracted to her—unless, of course, she was all decked out when he left. And let us add, that getting dressed is not slapping on sweat clothes!

Ladies, face it: it's a fact of life, and it's been treated like a big secret for generations, but men go by what they see, and they are always attracted to something. If you don't make sure they are being attracted to you, then you have to ask to whom or to what are they being attracted. Take care of your outward appearance. Have a bright countenance. Make sure your husband expresses his desire for you.

Likewise, men need to train themselves to express their attraction to their wives. As we've said before, it's easy to take each other for granted. So, whatever improvements you can make, however small, will make a huge difference in how your wife responds to you. If you do not express your attraction to your wife, she may give up on you, and if she gives up, the two of you are in serious trouble.

The seventh basic human need is time with others and time alone. Too many people overlook this critical area of need in their marriages. Everyone, married or single, needs time alone. We all need time to think, to regroup, to be refreshed and to reflect. We especially need time alone with God. This is a very important part of our lives. Time alone and with God are part of our spiritual and personal growth and development.

The way a couple can help each other have time alone is to be sensitive to one another. For example, if a couple has young children or babies, and the mother stays at home full-time, she needs time to herself. She's been listening to baby talk and probably answering zillions of questions from a toddler. Her husband needs to give her that time, take over with the kids at least once a week and let her get out of the house, let her go shopping or go out with friends. Women need to get away from the house and the chores and just go out.

And whether it's politically correct or not, it's true: a woman getting out and shopping or having lunch with friends—doing those things women like to do—is what makes her feminine. Women who spend all day at the office and all evening with the children are just not going to be as feminine as women who have some time alone during the day. Working all day and washing clothes until 11 p.m. does not make a sexy wife! Men, help your wife, especially if she works outside the home. Protect her. Help her find time to be alone.

Now, when husbands and wives do go out with friends to get away, it's very important who those friends are. First Corinthians 15:33 NIV says, **Do not be misled: "Bad company corrupts good character."** Someone who claims to be a Christian but does not live a Christ-like life is no friend for you. That's not the kind of fellowship either of you need.

Both of you need true Christian friends. Men especially need other Christian men to challenge them, to discuss goals and ambitions with and to spark new ideas for their vocation. Proverbs 27:17 says, **Iron sharpeneth iron; so a man sharpeneth the countenance of his friend.**

The eighth basic human need is peace. All of us need peace, and the only true Source of peace is Jesus. He said Himself in John 14:27, **Peace I leave with you, my peace I give**

unto you: not as the world giveth, give I unto you. Let not your heart be troubled, neither let it be afraid.

Too many people in the day in which we live try to find peace through escape. They escape through valium, or other prescription or nonprescription drugs. What do you think marijuana and cocaine are all about? Whatever the method of escape, legal or prescribed, no escape is godly. Escape is bondage. Peace is not.

True peace is identified in Galatians 5:22 as a fruit of the Spirit. It is developed as we spend time in God's Word and in prayer and learn to yield to who we are on the inside—indwelt by the Spirit of God Himself. True peace is not something we work up...it is something we give into, something we yield to and allow to manifest in our lives, in our minds and in our hearts.

Peace is not demonstrated by hiding from your family. It's not trying to escape. It's not staying in bed all day with the covers over your head to avoid answering the phone.

No, true peace develops an atmosphere of tranquility in your heart first, and then in your home.

The ninth and last basic human need we've identified is pride in one's life's associates. This is simply the name we've given to feeling proud of the people we have around us. We all want to feel proud to introduce our husband or wife to others. We all want to live lives so that when we invite friends over for dinner, we're not embarrassed...so that the husband is not embarrassed by the condition of the home, or the behavior of the children, or the way his wife looks. And no woman wants to be ashamed of her husband, or be embarrassed.

A common occurrence in this area that we have observed is how women are often humiliated in public by their husbands, because of the way he belittles her or talks down to her. What men ought to do is brag on their wives. If they'd just compliment her once a day, she'd blossom, and probably blossom into whatever it is he really desires her to be.

What men need to realize is that if they belittle their wives and put her down, what they are really doing is putting themselves down...because they're the one who picked her. So if you're putting your spouse down, all you're saying is that you were dumb in your choice.

The truth is that a man wants to be married to a woman of whom he can be proud. Proverbs 12:4 NIV says, **A wife of noble character is her husband's crown, but a disgraceful wife is like decay in his bones.** This verse is so true, even in our day. Regardless of what you may think, in the business world men are not just judged by their performance, but the world will also look at their wives to make their final assessment. Therefore, women have tremendous power. They have the power to help or hinder their husband's career, and their own future as well.

For example, when people discuss a man, they often bring up the subject of his wife. They may say, "What do you think of John? Have you met his wife? Wow, she's a doll."

Hopefully they won't say, "Hey, have you met the new guy, John? Isn't he a great guy? But what about his wife. I wonder how he got stuck with her."

Women, remember that.

Producing Everlasting Love

As we said earlier, the needs you or your spouse may have are as unique as you are. But these nine basic human needs are a great place to start in learning how to meet the true needs of your partner, and not just what you *think* his or her needs are.

Remember to set some time aside and ask your partner what his or her needs are. Listen with an open heart and mind. In fact, just listen. Commit to not talking or assessing or giving feedback on what they need. Just listen and create a safe environment in which they can be vulnerable and honest. Commit in your heart ahead of time you won't be defensive and you won't critique their needs in your mind or with your mouth.

True, everlasting love is unconditional love...just like God gives to each of us. Part of becoming more Christ-like is learning to give that same love to others—starting most importantly with those whom we love the most, our husband or wife.

SECTION 2

Becoming One Flesh

*Be completely humble and gentle; be patient,
bearing with one another in love. Make every effort
to keep the unity of the Spirit through the bond
of peace.*

                                        Ephesians 4:2-3 NIV

CHAPTER 3

Exploring God's Special Plan for Your Marriage

Your marriage involves far more than you and your spouse and the decision you made one day at the altar—or courthouse! You may have made that decision in your own human power, but whether you realize it or not, you entered into a covenant with the God of the universe, the God of all creation. And that means there's more substance and power to ensure your success than you ever dreamed possible!

You see, when you were saying, "I do," God was saying, "We will." The "we" is all three of you, including His unlimited resources. Because of that, God has a very special plan for each and every marriage. It's a plan of success that involves becoming one flesh, becoming one in spirit, in achievement and in purpose.

Let's study and explore this together.

In our day and age, we have all kinds of innovations in marriage. We have trial marriages, homosexual marriages, no-fault marriages and all kinds of other ideas. But, the best thing for us to do is look to God for His original purpose and intent for marriage.

Yes, God has an intention for your marriage. He has a divine purpose for your marriage, and everyone else's marriages. In fact, in Matthew 19:3, when Jesus began responding to the Pharisees' questions about divorce, He pressed them back to the roots of God's purpose for marriage and the family.

> Some Pharisees came to him to test him. They asked, "Is it lawful for a man to divorce his wife for any and every reason?"
>
> "Haven't you read," he replied, "that at the beginning the Creator 'made them male and female,' and said, 'For this reason a man will leave his father and mother and be united to his wife, and the two will become one flesh'? So they are no longer two, but one. Therefore what God has joined together, let man not separate."
>
> "Why then," they asked, "did Moses command that a man give his wife a certificate of divorce and send her away?"
>
> Jesus replied, "Moses permitted you to divorce your wives because your hearts were hard. But it was not this way from the beginning."
>
> Matthew 19:3-8 NIV

At the end of His answer, Jesus' remedy for divorce was not more rules and regulations, but the rediscovery of the eternal purpose for marriage. You see, Moses had permitted them to divorce their wives because their hearts were hard, but it was not meant to be that way in the beginning.

The Pharisees looked at life the way many married people do: "What can I get away with?" But God's way is to live our lives from a perspective that asks, "What is God's intention for my life?"

And just like your individual life, as we have said, God has a special intention for your marriage. He tells us the original purpose for marriage in Genesis 1:26-28 NIV:

> Then God said, "Let us make man in our image, in our likeness, and let them rule over the fish of the sea and the birds of the air, over the livestock, over all the earth, and over all the creatures that move along the ground."
>
> So God created man in his own image, in the image of God he created him; male and female he created them. God blessed them and said to them, "Be fruitful and increase in number; fill the earth and subdue it. Rule over the fish of the sea and the birds of the air and over every living creature that moves on the ground."

There is even more clarity concerning the purpose of marriage in chapter 2, verses 15-25 NIV:

> The LORD God took the man and put him in the Garden of Eden to work it and take care of it.
>
> And the LORD God commanded the man, "You are free to eat from any tree in the garden; but you must not eat from the tree of the knowledge of good and evil, for when you eat of it you will surely die."
>
> The LORD God said, "It is not good for the man to be alone. I will make a helper suitable for him."

Now the LORD God had formed out of the ground all the beasts of the field and all the birds of the air. He brought them to the man to see what he would name them; and whatever the man called each living creature, that was its name. So the man gave names to all the livestock, the birds of the air and all the beasts of the field. But for Adam no suitable helper was found.

So the LORD God caused the man to fall into a deep sleep; and while he was sleeping, he took one of the man's ribs and closed up the place with flesh. Then the LORD God made a woman from the rib he had taken out of the man, and he brought her to the man.

The man said, "This is now bone of my bones and flesh of my flesh; she shall be called 'woman,' for she was taken out of man." For this reason a man will leave his father and mother and be united to his wife, and they will become one flesh.

The man and his wife were both naked, and they felt no shame.

When you study these passages of scripture, you find several purposes for the covenant of marriage:

1. They were to rule–Genesis 1:26.
2. They were to be fruitful and increase–Genesis 1:28.
3. They were to be together–Genesis 2:18,24.

God's Threefold Plan for Your Marriage

These three purposes reveal God's threefold plan for your marriage. As we study each one, take hold of these as a foundation of success for your marriage. Examine where you need to reinforce your foundation or build up a corner of the building.

The first purpose God mentioned was to rule. Just like the first man and woman, we are called to rule in this life. To rule in this life requires a power between two partners, and the most powerful tool any married couple has is agreement.

As believers, we know this is true in prayer. Jesus Himself taught us about the power of agreement in Matthew 18:19-20 when He said, **Again I say unto you, That if two of you shall agree on earth as touching any thing that they shall ask, it shall be done for them of my Father which is in heaven. For where two or three are gathered together in my name, there am I in the midst of them.**

Because believers know the power of agreement in prayer, they often will search out someone to pray with them and agree for their request. Well, who better to be in agreement with than your husband or wife?

There is a formidable power between a husband and a wife who are joined in agreement. There is a power among them and between them to rule. To rule over what? Over whatever is coming against their marriage, their home, their children, or against one of them as individuals, perhaps from a situation in their job.

So there's a great resource of strength in the marriage relationship that is in agreement. But when we allow strife, which is disagreement, to come in, then we lose that power of our partnership. James 3:16 tells us, **For where envying and strife is, there is confusion and every evil work.** In other words, where there is strife and division, the dominion that marriage actually affords to married partners is negated.

While we were living in Kenya, a situation arose that illustrates the importance of being in agreement. Actually, Gene and I were in the middle of an argument when a crisis arose with our six-month-old son, Austin. When he was just a little guy, he used to love to sit in my lap and pull the combs out of my hair. He also had another habit, one that is common to all small children. When he became tired, he would rub his eyes. Well, on that day and in the midst of that argument, we heard Austin scream out in pain. Since he was on my lap all along, I couldn't for the life of me figure out what he had done to himself. Gene and I looked him over, and to our horror we discovered that he had become tired and rubbed his eyes while he had one of the combs from my hair in his hand. Across one of his beautiful green eyes there were a series of deep gashes from the comb.

To make a long story short, we took him to an opthamologist in Nairobi after unsuccessfully taking him to the Nairobi Hospital. The opthamologist said that Austin had scratched his eye so deeply that he nearly pierced the eye which would have resulted in instant blindness. Even though the eye had not been pierced, the doctor said that the cornea would heal with scar tissue and his eyesight would forever be blighted.

We took Austin home that afternoon, applied the medicine and did the best we could to hold him, comfort him and love on him. But more than anything we repented to God and to each other for allowing ourselves to get into strife. We got back into agreement fast! Then every time Austin cried in pain and every time we were tempted to worry, we would speak the Word of God over his life and over his eyes.

The next day the opthamologist said it was a miracle. The eye was almost totally healed, and with no scar tissue. A week later the doctor confirmed that the healing was complete, again with no scar tissue. Now all these years have passed and our son's eyesight is normal in every way and there has never been any scar tissue or any other evidence of that terrible afternoon.

But what did remain was our conviction that strife carries too great a price since it leaves an open door for the enemy to come in. Now, we make every effort to remain in constant agreement, together, upon God's unchanging Word.

—Sue

Satan himself is out to destroy the power of agreement in marriages. Strife is his tool to destroy the unity in marriages and create great divisions and gulfs in relationships. As believers and married couples, we've got to be determined that we will not let anyone or anything separate our unity.

It is important to understand that God didn't just intend for Adam and Eve to rule; He intended for them to rule together. They were created to rule as a team.

You see, marriage is God's plan to show the kind of unity that He has established between Christ and the church. Therefore, when a Christian husband and wife are really operating as a team, you should see in their marriage a microcosm of what the relationship is like between Christ and the church.

But here's the exciting and even more powerful part of our unity. When we are united in God's covenant of marriage, there are not really just two of us in agreement, there are actually three working together: the husband, the wife and the Holy Spirit—the very Spirit of God Himself.

You can't get more power to succeed than that. When you have God in the midst of your relationship, you are destined to succeed in every area of life!

The true object of agreement is not to just walk in agreement as a husband and wife—although that is powerful and good—but it is to walk in agreement and unity with God. That is the best way to live your life altogether. That is His will and it is confirmed in His Word. Ecclesiastes 4:12 NIV tells us, **Though one may be overpowered, two can defend themselves. A cord of three strands is not quickly broken.**

Three in agreement. That is the way to live your married life. With teamwork—and God on the team—you will have greater success than you ever imagined.

Abounding in Fruitfulness

The second purpose in God's threefold plan for your marriage is to be fruitful and increase, or multiply. People always associate this with having children, but God was talking in a much broader fashion. He was talking about a growing, developing relationship. If a marriage is growing, there is total well-being in the relationship. God wanted the coming together of the man and the woman to lead to fruitfulness. That means that together, they were to be more productive than when they were single. They were to experience the blessing of the Lord upon their marriage. That blessing of the Lord manifests as prosperity in every area: fruitfulness in finances, fruitfulness emotionally, fruitfulness vocationally and so on. It is a fruitfulness in greater power between the two than each of them could have ever achieved individually.

They were not to just increase by having children, but they were to increase in every area of life. God wants every marriage—including yours—to be growing, fruitful and productive. He wants each year for you to increase more than all the previous years of your married life, and not just during the childbearing years.

It's possible you've never heard that God wants you to increase and be successful. But that is His will. That is the truth. He loves you and wants the absolute best for you. He's on your side. He is for you and not against you. And He's for your marriage being all you ever dreamed it could be.

Ever since the book of Genesis, it has been the will of God that every person be successful, that they be fruitful and increase. Unfortunately though, our generation, more than any other, has discovered the fastest and surest way to decrease and *not* be fruitful. That way is divorce.

You simply cannot increase and go through a divorce. Divorce is a sure way to decrease in every area. And divorce is a prime cause of poverty in the United States, because when you divide assets, force the sale of your home and pay for attorneys—for starters—you are not headed down the road to prosperity. The only ones who win in divorces are the lawyers—they are the ones who become rich!

Divorce is a thief in every way. It even robs children of their rightful inheritance. That's why every generation in the United States—where one out of every two marriages ends in divorce—is always starting over. They are always starting over with nothing, starting from scratch, and even in debt because there is nothing left to pass on down to them.

Husbands and wives, you need to realize that when you fail in your marriage, you aren't only robbing yourselves, you are robbing your children of what is rightfully theirs.

The Joy of Companionship

The third purpose of God's threefold plan for your marriage is that you are to be together. Being together is simply the joy of companionship with one another. For us, we love getting away together. We love to bring in Sue's mom to keep the kids, and we just go off without them. It's wonderful. Sometimes we've felt guilty about that. But over the years, we've learned that the kids are always there when we get back! So we might as well go and enjoy ourselves on occasion.

God wants us to do things like that. In Genesis 2:18 and 24, the Word indicates that the man and the woman weren't just created and then put together to procreate. No, they were created and put together to be together...to spend time together, to enjoy the company of one another. Adam and Eve's marriage was not just to legitimize the birthing of children, but to allow them the privilege of enjoying one another's company.

You see, God never intended for us to exist apart from others. We are not designed to exist in an isolated state. Despite what literature records, no man is truly an island to himself. The truth is, the only place we can find fulfillment in this life is in relationships with other people, and our closest relationship is in our relationship of marriage.

All three of these plans were created to work together in your marriage: the plan of ruling, the plan of being fruitful and multiplying and the plan of being together. If you have identified ones that are not operating in your marriage, then begin developing those skills in your marriage by practicing them just like you've practiced and mastered other skills in your life. The blessings that will follow will improve your own life and the life of your marriage.

God's Intention for Equality

As we mentioned at the beginning of the chapter, Adam and Eve were put in the garden to be together and to function together in complete harmony. They were created to be a team, and on a team everyone's value is equal.

Most people have heard teaching and instruction, as well as political rhetoric, on the ever-popular debate of whether men and woman are equal or not. What confuses most people is that they don't understand the difference between quality versus function.

Many people will cite Ephesians 5, where it states in verses 22-24, **Wives, submit yourselves unto your own husbands, as unto the Lord. For the husband is the head of the wife, even as Christ is the head of the church: and he is the saviour of the body. Therefore as the church is subject unto Christ, so let the wives be to their own husbands in every thing,** and they interpret from this that there is a difference in quality between men and women, but there is not.

Now, there is a difference in function, but not in quality. Men are not superior to women, and women are not superior to men. Likewise, men are not inferior to women, and women are not inferior to men. Well, what are they, then? They have equal value, or equality, in the eyes of God, but they have different functions.

To understand this more easily, consider the transmission and the engine in your car. Both are required for your car to run. Therefore, they both have the same value to you. But one is not more important than the other, because both are essential to the success of driving your car.

In the same way, the man and woman have different functions, but they are both essential and have the same value.

The function of a woman is not the same as the function of a man. Nonetheless, they are of equal value in the eyes of God. The passage in Ephesians 5 is talking about function, not value. Therefore, it's important to understand that how you see yourself and your mate—as superior, inferior or equal—can have a tremendous impact on the potential success of your marriage.

For example, as we've stated in earlier chapters, there are many factors that affect an individual's chance of success in marriage: their relationship with God, their childhood upbringing, their socioeconomic status before marriage, their reasons for marrying and so on. We've talked about how important it is to have a healthy self-esteem, a healthy self-image, and how when one partner doesn't have that proper self-image, they will put the other down to try and make up for their lack of self-esteem.

But there is something else that will work against your success in marriage and the companionship God intended for your marriage, and it is directly related to how you view the equality of you and your spouse. That something else is pride, or arrogance. Pride, or arrogance, is simply thinking more highly of yourself than you ought.

So, in marriage, your view of equality can be distorted in two ways. One, if you don't think well of yourself, you try to pull everyone else down to your level. And two, if you think more highly of yourself than you should, you'll still be putting people down because you will view them as being inferior. Both are wrong, and neither incorporate God's view of the man and the woman. His value of each of them is the same.

None of us should ever have the idea that we are superior to our spouse, that we're better than they are. Yes, it's very likely that you do things differently, look at things differently and approach situations differently. That's probably because you were raised in different parts of the country, came from different backgrounds and families, and were taught different perspectives of life. But now you are married. And marriage requires you to become one in partnership in order to succeed.

Becoming ONE in Your Partnership

Whether you realize it or not, there is an objective that God created and intended for your marriage. It's part of the purpose of your marriage. God intended for the two of you to become one. The biblical term is "one flesh."

In Genesis 2:23-25, Adam explained the concept of "one flesh:"

> **And Adam said, This is now bone of my bones, and
> flesh of my flesh: she shall be called Woman, because**

she was taken out of Man. Therefore shall a man leave his father and his mother, and shall cleave unto his wife: and they shall be one flesh. And they were both naked, the man and his wife, and were not ashamed.

Now, we're going to explain the meaning of this passage thoroughly before this chapter concludes, but first let us encourage you that "oneness" doesn't happen on the wedding night. Yes, you become one flesh according to the biblical concept, but true oneness develops over a lifetime. It is a process. For example, when you meet someone, you don't become intimate with that person in a one-night stand, or in an initial encounter. No, it takes time to get to know one another. True intimacy takes place over time, and the greatest intimacy that a man and woman will ever have between them will be that intimacy that takes place day after day, month after month and year after year. But that takes commitment.

And God created it this way. He made marriage three-dimensional. It is a union of Himself, man and woman, and the coming together of these three creates the desired oneness of covenant. Because of this union, marriage belongs to God. It's His plan for man. That's why it is so important when we enter into marriage to understand that to receive the benefits from the marriage relationship, we must fulfill the duties and obligations God intended for us to accomplish.

We can't play God and make all the decisions. We can't just decide one day that we want to be in a marriage and the next day we want out. No, we need to put forth the same effort and initiative into having a successful marriage and working at oneness as we would in any other endeavor in life. We have to be committed to the success of our marriages.

We live in a society where everyone wants the fruit, but they don't want to tend the vineyard. They want the gratification, but they don't want to toil and put forth the necessary labor.

What we need to wake up to and realize is that when we say "I do" to one another, we're not just saying "yes" to each other, but we're also saying "yes" to God.

Because marriage belongs to God, because it's His plan, because He has a specific purpose for each and every union, we simply cannot go into our marriages, do our own thing and then expect to be successful in it.

If we want our marriage to work and be prosperous and fruitful, we have to wake up and allow God to be a part of the covenant we've made, especially since the covenant of marriage belongs to Him anyway!

Even though a man and woman may take their marriage and do whatever they want to with it, it still belongs to God. They won't reap God's results and God's blessings in their relationship, in their home and in their family that way, but their union is God's regardless.

God's plan for marriage is a union that is enduring and indissoluble, not something that breaks up for any and every reason.

We often counsel young people about the importance of being equally yoked in marriage based on what the apostle Paul wrote to the Church in Second Corinthians 6:14: **Be ye not unequally yoked together with unbelievers: for what fellowship hath righteousness with unrighteousness? and what communion hath light with darkness?** Many times, however, they don't want to listen. Too many times couples marry for the wrong reasons: They want to escape from home, escape from mom and dad, escape the pressures of school or escape having to make a living. Somehow they think married life will be easier than the life in which they're living. Little do they know the work and effort required to become one flesh, the work and effort required to enter into the covenant of marriage God's way.

Three Practical Steps to Achieving One Flesh

As we read earlier in Genesis, chapter 2, the Word says that the man and woman, meaning Adam and Eve, were naked, but they felt no shame. Immediately, we tend to relate that to the physical realm.

But what about the other arenas in life? What about the emotional realm? Can you stand before your spouse emotionally naked and feel no shame? What about vocationally? Is it possible for you personally to let your husband or wife know all of your career goals and feel no shame? Are you afraid to do so for fear you won't achieve them all?

If you feel this way, or in other ways you feel inhibited from being completely vulnerable to your spouse, then what is being revealed is an area where you need to become one flesh. See, one flesh doesn't just refer to the physical union, but also it means a coming together over time where we're more unified now than we were last year—and not just physically, but emotionally, vocationally, spiritually—virtually in every area.

Husbands and wives need to have the freedom and security in their marriage relationship to share their highest goals, deepest fears and expectations with their partner. This won't happen if there is an undercurrent of the possibility that one or the other will be laughed at, made fun of, scoffed at, put down or belittled. If you can't share with your spouse on the intimate level you deeply desire, then as a team you need to grow in being emotionally naked before one another, and thus become more one in this most intimate area of sharing and loving in marriage.

From all we've taught you thus far, we're sure you're catching on that becoming one flesh is really the ultimate goal for your marriage, and it is a process you live out all of your married life. To help you get on the right track in this area, the following are three steps to achieving one flesh in marriage: severance, permanence and unity.

The first step is severance.

Severing something is the act of cutting through so that there are two, and one goes one way and the other goes another way. It means leaving. In Genesis 2:24, which we mentioned earlier, we find an instruction regarding severing: **Therefore shall a man leave his father and his mother, and shall cleave unto his wife: and they shall be one flesh.**

This is what we call the "leave-cleave principle." It is a severing from the mother and father, and a cleaving to the new spouse. Sometimes it can be a severing of geographic locations, and that's a good idea. (It's not usually good to live with mom or dad...or next door!) But it is definitely an emotional severance, and emotional separation. The things that a young couple once looked to receive from their parents—finances, emotional support, meals, clean laundry, guidance, direction—must now come from one another.

This means you solve your difficulties together. You support one another in the relationship. The husband takes on the function as head of the household and chief provider. The wife takes on the function of being wife and helper to her husband. They go from the roles of a son and a daughter to the roles of a husband and a wife.

Your relationship with your parents is a new one. This doesn't mean you forget about, disregard or dishonor them in any way. But you and your spouse are a new family, and as different as it is from what you've been accustomed to, you have to honor one another above the extended family–yes, mom and dad are now extended family–and become one. Women need to look to their husbands to fulfill their financial and emotional needs. And men need to look to their wives for advice and counsel. In other words, your loyalties have to change. Your first loyalty now has to be your husband or wife, and your secondary loyalty is to your parents.

So to make the marriage successful, both the husband and the wife have to be willing to separate themselves from their parents–leave–and separate themselves unto their new husband or wife–cleave. It's making a decision to become one and it requires a cutting of the emotional umbilical cord with mom and dad.

Marriage, particularly with young people, is unlike anything they've ever done before. It's not just a commitment or a promise, it's a covenant–a covenant with God that belongs to God. It's a whole new ball game. It's not a car payment, or a contract to pay apartment rent. It's not like anything they've known. It's no longer relating day by day to mom and dad. It's relating day by day to husband or to wife. And as long as either of you runs home to Mama– regardless of your age or how long you've been married– then there will not be a coming together in the marriage.

Now, we said Mama because it's not generally the women who run home...it's the men who run home to Mama. They even say to their wives, "You can't cook like Mama. You don't do my shirts like Mama. Mama always sewed on my buttons!"

That's really when wives need to say, "Well, hush your mouth!"

So step number one is, in essence, "Don't run home to Mama!" which translates to severance—or leaving and cleaving. If you leave and cleave, you'll have a much better chance at attaining step number two.

The second step is permanence.

Part of a couples leaving and cleaving to one another is their making a commitment to the marriage that is permanent. If both genuinely leave and cleave, then there is a dual commitment to the marriage, which results in becoming one flesh. That dual commitment is a commitment by each partner to the other partner and to the marriage itself.

It has to be dual. You can't be committed to your mate but not to the marriage. No, that won't work. It has to be to both. And that dual commitment and becoming one flesh yield a sense of permanence for the marriage.

This commitment to marriage is not, "Well, I'm going to try it." No, there are no loopholes. There just can't be if you want permanence. If you want to succeed at anything, your commitment cannot have a short fuse. It must be a true, permanent commitment. It means that you say to your husband and wife, and they know it's true by your actions, that you will be there today and tomorrow, that you are more committed to them than you are to your parents or any other human being on the face of the earth.

It is this kind of special commitment that yields permanence and feelings of security in the relationship. And over time, it increases oneness.

The third step is unity.

Over time—remember, it's a process—as a couple leaves and cleaves and commits to the marriage, there is a growing together. And as there is a growing together, there is greater and greater unity between the husband and wife. There is actually the creation of a new family unit and a new way of looking at your relationship with yourself.

Your relationship with yourself is actually your own commitment to personal growth. It is important in the marriage relationship to keep growing—spiritually, mentally, emotionally, in every way. You've made a covenant commitment to another person, you've severed your old relationship with your parents and now you've committed to permanence and unity. Because you've committed to unity, you have to be committed to growth.

This means you have to be so committed to your husband or wife, that: 1) you allow room for them to grow. And 2) you make sure you are growing as well.

Growing in marriage is fun. It's an adventure. It's a wonderful, fulfilling, lifetime relationship when you do it according to God's plans and purposes for your marriage. If any of the purposes in this chapter have pricked your heart because you don't know how to successfully execute them, then just pray. Ask God to help you. Whether it's in the area of leaving and cleaving, not putting down your partner or nurturing the joy of companionship God intended for you to have, God will help you change and overcome. First John 4:4 says **Greater is he that is in you....** You can succeed. If you're a believer, then you've made Jesus the Lord of your life. That means His Spirit, the Spirit of the living God, is inside of you. And if you call on the Holy Spirit to help you, He is already commissioned and committed to helping you succeed. You are a winner in every area of your life!

CHAPTER 4

Achieving Unity in Your Marriage

Becoming one flesh in marriage is like living out the specific adventure God created just for you and your mate. It's a wonderful lifelong experience of teaming up to achieve visions, goals and dreams.

How smooth your individual journey is during all the years of married life can depend on a number of factors—particularly how unified you are and how skilled you are in your day-to-day roles in interacting. Just like everyone on a baseball team or a football team has to fulfill a role for the team as a whole to succeed and win, so do a husband and wife need to fulfill their roles for the marriage to succeed and win throughout the course of life.

You see, people can stand around all day talking about their philosophies and opinions about marriage. They can talk about what constitutes a marriage, who should be married, why people should marry and what "really" makes a successful marriage.

But if you are married, then you know the nuts and bolts of married life are not in vain musings, but in what happens every day...it's how you relate to each other and what roles you live out in your day-to-day interaction. And any marriage that is going to be successful is going to require the fulfillment of certain roles.

Before we get into examining all the possible nuts and bolts about marital roles, let's review what we've learned thus far about the origin of marriage and cover some of its history right up to the present day. Knowing the origin of and God's purpose for marriage makes the nuts and bolts fall into place.

We've learned that marriage originated with God. He created the covenant of marriage for mankind, and He created it to be permanent. He created it for man and woman to rule together and be fruitful. He created it for companionship and oneness.

Now, in American culture, as we mentioned in the last chapter, there are many innovations in marriage, such as trial marriages, homosexual marriages, no-fault marriages and so on. But none of those kinds of marriages were around when marriage originated in the mind of God. The only kind of marriage that was from the beginning of time was a man and a woman joined by a covenant with each other and with God Himself–a covenant created to last a lifetime.

So, God created the covenant of marriage for man and woman. But the interesting thing about this is that the covenant of marriage wasn't for each individual man and woman alone.

That's because whether we realize it or not, what happens in marriages affects those around us. It affects our society, our culture. And the opposite is true; what happens in our society and culture affects our marriages. This is all because the covenant of marriage is an institution. That doesn't sound very glamorous, but it's true. The fact is, the quality of a society's marriages affects the quality of that society as a whole.

As modern day people living in a free nation, we are living in a throw-away society. Rather than seeing the family unit as being the basic building block of society, we have entered into this "do your own thing" generation. Many of the results are obvious. For example, because of the number of divorces and torn-up families, we now see orphaned and alienated young people on the streets of our nation joining gangs so they can have some semblance of a family. Unfortunately, divorce has accelerated our modern cultural and moral decline. As families have weakened and failed, so has our culture faltered.

In contrast, we can look back a generation or two to our grandmother's day and see how the most important aspect about a marriage was simply staying together. The emphasis was not placed on enjoying the marriage back then, but rather on child-rearing, responsibility and duty.

Now, not all of these emphases are bad. They lent to a strong and stable society, but our culture has changed—in some good ways and some bad. Today, such concepts as "stability" and "commitment" are like dirty words to us. When people talk of the priorities in a marriage as staying together out of a sense of duty or rearing children, we think they should wash their mouths out with soap!

But in our grandmother's day, marriage was a commitment—and that's good. And today, we know we can have fun in our marriages. We can have enjoyment in our marriages. But the truth we sometimes neglect is that we can only really fully experience the enjoyment and the fun if we're willing to make it a lifelong commitment, and nothing less.

So many of our modern society's views, unlike our grandmother's generation, are influenced by the media, and the big emphasis everywhere—from children's shows to primetime television—is on individual rights and personal happiness. From the time a child watches Big Bird on PBS or goes off to school, it's being pounded into them that if they are not enjoying a particular activity, then they can simply walk off. They can leave it, call it quits and in essence, pick up their marbles and go home.

So as adults, we are a generation that has grown up thinking that someone else is responsible for our happiness. The world system would have us believe that if we're not happy, then we should go find somebody who will make us happy. But that is not reality.

Whenever there are problems in a marriage, whenever one of the partners is unhappy, that partner doesn't seem to realize that personal happiness is his or her own individual responsibility. To say to your spouse, "I'm just not happy," is to say to them, "You are responsible for making me happy"—and that is simply not the truth.

No, the truth is, you are responsible for making yourself happy. You are responsible because happiness comes from within yourself. When you find your happiness coming from within, then you aren't dependent on your surroundings for contentment. You have found the source of happiness that keeps you happy regardless of what your partner or anyone else around you is doing.

Rather than wasting the best years of your life looking for someone who will make you happy, why not decide you are going to be happy, that you are going to be full of the joy of the Lord? Why not decide today that you are going to develop that joy and that happiness in your life to its fullest potential?

When you get right down to it, that's what we're really talking about. We're talking about taking on the responsibility to get out of your marriage what you feel you want out of it—including happiness and everything else you want.

But to do this, there's one very important key to your ultimate success, and it is essential. You have to go to God's Word to find what makes a marriage successful. This is not something you attempt in your flesh with your own natural knowledge. That will get you so far, but not to your ultimate destination of true happiness.

The Nuts and Bolts

While marriage is an institution, and there is merit in maintaining your marriage for the sake of its importance to yourselves, your children and others, it is vitally important that the two individuals within the marriage feel they are receiving something from the relationship, something wholesome, something good. Each partner needs to feel that they are growing and maturing as individuals.

One way to accomplish such a marriage that is flourishing in mutual fulfillment is to walk in the roles God created for the husband and wife as outlined in His Word. In our marriage, for example, we have discovered over the years that conflicts generally revolve around the division of labor and the decision-making process. In other words, it centers on the nuts and bolts of day-to-day living—who will take out the trash, who will handle the money, who will write the checks, who will cash the checks, who will handle the tax return.

A lot of times in marriages, the husband will be pinching pennies regarding the wife's weekly budget, and he'll be demanding this and demanding that, but then one day he'll come home in a brand new Corvette! There is definitely something wrong in this household's decision-making process!

The wife is thinking, *Here I am sacrificing and scrimping, and who's making all the decisions about where the money goes?*

Now, we didn't use this illustration because we believe the man ought to always handle the money. Sometimes in a family the wife is simply more adept at handling the finances. That's not the point of the illustration. The point is unity.

In fact, a successful marriage not only means a commitment to unity, but also a commitment to continuing that relationship. That means continuing to come together to achieve an understanding of the decision-making process and the division of labor.

This actually demands a commitment to fulfilling the roles as outlined by the apostle Paul in Ephesians 5:21-33 NIV:

> **Submit to one another out of reverence for Christ. Wives, submit to your husbands as to the Lord. For the husband is the head of the wife as Christ is the head of the church, his body, of which he is the Savior.**

Now as the church submits to Christ, so also wives should submit to their husbands in everything. Husbands, love your wives, just as Christ loved the church and gave himself up for her to make her holy, cleansing her by the washing with water through the word, and to present her to himself as a radiant church, without stain or wrinkle or any other blemish, but holy and blameless.

In this same way, husbands ought to love their wives as their own bodies. He who loves his wife loves himself. After all, no one ever hated his own body, but he feeds and cares for it, just as Christ does the church–for we are members of his body. "For this reason a man will leave his father and mother and be united to his wife, and the two will become one flesh." This is a profound mystery–but I am talking about Christ and the church.

However, each one of you also must love his wife as he loves himself, and the wife must respect her husband.

The apostle Paul is using a metaphor here for illustration, but there is a limit to the application. The point we are to get is this: Wives are to submit to their husbands as the church submits to Christ, our Lord; and husbands are to love their wives as Christ loved the church. For example, the husband loving his wife and his wife submitting to and loving her husband should not result in behavior that violates a higher loyalty–our loyalty to God. So "submission" to one's husband should not lead to illegal or immoral behavior. The wife can only rightly submit to her husband as unto Christ, which always means legal and moral conduct.

So what does all this mean in our everyday roles? That there is a **helpmate** and there is a **head**. Those are the two primary roles Paul outlined, and the two roles we will define in this chapter. We'll begin with what it means to be a helpmate, and what it does not mean to be a helpmate.

In Genesis 1, when God said He would make a helpmate for Adam, the Hebrew word used for "helpmate" is *ezer*. This is the same word used in Psalm 121:1-2 NIV where it says, **I lift up my eyes to the hills—where does my help come from? My help comes from the LORD, the Maker of heaven and earth.**

In this scripture *ezer* is used concerning the Lord, speaking about the Lord. If you study the Bible, you will find *ezer* is often used, describing God as our Helper. So helpmate in no way signifies a second-class citizen. If God is your Helper, then "helper" cannot mean "second-class."

But sometimes in a marriage, a man will go to a seminar, hear this great revelation about how his wife is his helper, and come home telling her how she's supposed to be his helpmate...in a way that implies she is his servant, gopher, slave or whatever he deems it to be.

But God has an entirely different picture of this word "helpmate" and the role of one. He uses this term to refer to Himself, as we saw in Psalm 121. King David called God his helpmate. So from these references and many others, we know that the woman is a helpmate in the same way God is a helpmate, or an *ezer*. Further, what this tells us is that she is an essential part and partner in helping her husband be and become what he ought to be. She is a vital part of his achieving his maximum potential in life.

In fact, without her assistance in his life, he is not going to be, and he's not going to do, all that he could. There isn't any way it can happen, no more than it can happen without God's help.

The second role Paul outlined was that of the head. Just as there are misconceptions about what it means to be a helpmate, there are misconceptions about what it means to be the head of a home. Being the head does not mean being a dictator or some kind of perfect superman who can make no mistakes. Neither does it mean being a tyrant.

> *I know, regarding Sue being my helpmate, that there is no way, absolutely no way that I could be where I am today...having obtained my doctorate, being in our church that we pioneered in 1984, being on television in all 50 states, having no debt whatsoever...there is just no way I could have ever done any of it if I had married somebody other than Sue.*
> —Gene

No, headship means leadership, and leadership means that you have to solicit the cooperation of others in order to achieve a common goal.

When a man acts like a leader instead of a tyrant, then his wife can submit to him with a whole heart. Truthfully, you can't make someone submit. Submission is strictly voluntary. And the only way to get someone, namely your wife, to submit to you is to become the man that God intended you to be. By being the head and the sacrificial, loving leader of your family that God called you to be, you will woo her into submitting to your leadership. In other words, if you will lovingly lead, your family will respectfully follow.

Paul exhorted husbands in Ephesians 5:25 NIV to **love your wives, just as Christ loved the church and gave himself**

up for her. So the function of headship is not to be the boss, but to love through sacrificial leadership. If you want to be the head, then you have to be the one to give to your family. Headship isn't driving a family like you drive cattle. Headship means to get out in front of everyone else and to lovingly and sacrificially lead the family by example, just as Christ leads His church.

The apostle Paul also said that the husband is the head of the wife even as Christ is the Head of the church. Well, how is Christ the Head of the church? He lovingly gave up His life for His church. Christ leads His church through loving leadership. He solicits obedience, the submission and the cooperation of the church, through His love.

This book is full of information and revelation from God's Word on how to make your marriage successful, but when you get right down to it, our success in marriage is dependent on our being Christ-like and being willing to be like Christ in His dealings with the church, by laying down of our lives for one another.

Let's look at Ephesians 5:33 NIV one more time: **However, each one of you also must love his wife as he loves himself, and the wife must respect her husband.**

The husband is to love his wife, and the wife is to respect her husband. Husbands, you are to love your wives as you love yourselves. Truly, the key for Ephesians 5 to work in your marriage does not lie with the wife, but with the husband. So if there's a breakdown with Ephesians 5 happening in your marriage, the burden of responsibility to correct the situation is on the man. Why? Because respect has to be earned. Husbands are to love their wives and live with them in such a way as to win their respect. That's when things will fall into order in your home.

This very same principle applies to your children, as well. The apostle Paul says fathers are not to embitter their children, lest they discourage them (Colossians 3:21). Did you know that you can actually discipline a child in such a way that you will automatically embitter that child–and whether or not that child becomes embittered is not the responsibility of the child? No, it's the responsibility of the father and how he disciplines. So as a father, you have to earn your child's respect, and how you discipline them is a key to that. For example, one way to embitter a child is to embarrass, humiliate or belittle them publicly in front of others, especially their peers. Another way is to be overly harsh, which crushes the soul and saddens the heart. Discipline should always be fair and just and administered with love and understanding.

Both the husband and father roles require a man to be a sacrificial, loving leader in the home. A man does this specifically by his conversation, attitude and conduct. A man is to elicit, or woo, the voluntary cooperation of his wife and family.

Contrary to this, if a man loses his family's respect, especially if he loses it through sexual immorality, he has no right to ask God to forgive him and then go home and instantly expect his family to respect him as they did before. Why is that? Because the family learned to respect him by faith. They had no reason to doubt him. But now he has proven them wrong, and so he has to pull double duty, so to speak, to win their respect again. A man in this situation has to realize he has proven himself dishonorable...and it takes double duty on his part to win respect a second time.

Now, on the other hand, a wife dealing with this situation shouldn't make it impossible for the man, nor should she refuse to forgive him. But the process of the wife and children learning to respect the husband and father again will take time. The husband will have to invest time now in order to win back the respect of his wife and children.

The Meaning of Real Submission

We've already stated that submission is a voluntary act and that you can't make someone submit. We've talked about how submission requires respect and particularly how a husband has to earn the respect of his wife and family. But let's go a little deeper concerning our understanding of submission.

The word "submit" in the Greek language means "to voluntarily lift up." It does not mean to pull down or to put one down. Therefore, when you submit to someone, you voluntarily lift that person up. Ephesians 5:19-21 NIV says, **Speak to one another with psalms, hymns and spiritual songs. Sing and make music in your heart to the Lord, always giving thanks to God the Father for everything, in the name of our Lord Jesus Christ. Submit to one another out of reverence for Christ.** So if we abide by the Word of God according to Ephesians 5:21, we'll submit to one another in our marriages.

By submitting to one another, we will voluntarily lift each other up. So if you're lifting up your husband or wife in submission to them, and your spouse is also lifting you up in submission to you, then you're both lifting up each other, and no one is putting anyone down.

This is the mutual submission that God intended to be in every marriage. If you persist in the practice of continually lifting one another up in submission to one another, all you will do is go up and up and up and up. And then you have a wonderful, mutually fulfilling, successful marriage.

And you know the opposite situation. If you have a couple that is continually putting one another down and is not in submission to each other, they are going down, down, down.

Genesis 1:27 says, **So God created man in his own image, in the image of God created he him; male and female created he them.** And as we said in chapter 3, there is a difference in function between the husband and the wife, between the head and the helpmate, but there is not a difference in value. They have both been created in the image of God. Therefore, the image of God is both in the male and the female. Both roles have the same value. Both roles are just as essential.

Learning your God-given role is critical to harmony and unity in your home. As we said once before, based on James 3:16, where there is strife and contention, there will be every evil work. And in First Peter 3:7, we know it will hinder our prayers: **Likewise, ye husbands, dwell with them according to knowledge, giving honour unto the wife, as unto the weaker vessel, and as being heirs together of the grace of life; that your prayers be not hindered.**

You see, your marriage was meant by God to be a wonderful and blissful time of companionship, togetherness and agreement. And in that agreement, the level of your corporate faith as a husband and wife in unity, will just be ever-increasing and ever-exploding. Your marriage, unlike marriages in your grandmother's generation, is not just a matter of procreation or duty or obligation. It is much higher. We all have to get a vision for what God wanted in our marriages from the beginning. When we grasp that from His Word and apply it, then we will have the ideal marriage God created for us to have.

As husbands and wives increasingly become one flesh together and more unified, then their faith to overcome in life will have greater power. As we grow together in love and unity, in submission, in lovingly leading and lovingly submitting, our marriages will become God's best and exactly what He had in mind for us all along.

SECTION 3

Solving the Mystery of Effective Communication

Let no corrupt communication proceed out of your mouth, but that which is good to the use of edifying, that it may minister grace unto the hearers.

Ephesians 4:29

CHAPTER 5

The Power of Listening and Loving

Communication is talked about as *the* key in all interpersonal relationships. Whether it's between workers and managers, teachers and students or simply best friends, communication seems to be this big mystery everyone tries to solve and master. Well, it's no different in a marriage. Husbands and wives have to master communication in marriage just like they do in other relationships to be successful.

But unlike other interpersonal relationships, such as the one you have with your boss, your relationship with your husband or wife has a tremendous edge. It has the foundation of love, and that is one of the two greatest secrets to successful communication that we are going to cover in this chapter.

Colossians 4:6 NIV says, **Let your conversation be always full of grace....** Full of grace means gracious. When we are gracious to our partners in our communication, we are listening and we are loving.

So many times in a marriage this kind of graciousness is not given. Instead, two monologues are spoken. Rather than listening while one partner is speaking, the listener is actually thinking about how he or she is going to respond as soon as it's his or her turn to talk. The problem with this kind of behavior is not poor listening on the part of the spouse who's supposed to be listening—the problem is actually that no listening is taking place at all! Nothing can be resolved from this kind of behavior.

A dialogue, however, is different. In a dialogue two people are sharing—and listening. When you have two people in a marriage who are committed to dialogue, which means two-way conversation, they truly can work out any problem. If two people have committed their lives to Christ, to each other and subsequently to dialogue, then there is no problem in their marriage that they can't work out.

So if communication has been a challenge in your marriage, you need to refine or develop two very important skills: listening and loving.

Defining Your New Skills

There are many misconceptions in our technological society about what, exactly, listening and loving really are. Contrary to what we may have come to believe, listening has nothing to do with the high technology equipment we have in our homes or cars! In fact, telling your wife she can page you if she needs you is not communication. Just because we have telephones, digital pagers, car phones and fax machines does not mean we are communicating!

Quite the contrary, listening and loving in communication is not only the sharing or giving of information, but it is also the process of receiving information. For example, if you send a piece of information to your wife, it is not communication until the message is received. Likewise, anyone could pick up the telephone, dial numbers at random, and carry on half an hour of conversation with mom or dad, but that does not mean communication took place unless you dialed the right numbers, and unless mom or dad actually picked up on the other end and received what you had to say. So communication is not communication unless there is both sharing and receiving of information.

Listening and loving revolve around this key aspect of giving and receiving. If you're giving out information, you will have to be receiving information as well. If you aren't, then you are having a one-sided conversation, which is a monologue. When you're actively engaged in listening and loving, someone is giving the message, and someone is receiving the message. This exchange is rooted in respect.

We've talked about respect several times in this book, but it is so critical to every area of your marriage. When you have the crucial element of mutual respect in your communication, then you are going to spend time communicating. You're going to spend quality time and a quantity of time together. For example, it is just not good enough for a husband to say, "Well, I'm going to give you five minutes of quality time this evening, dear." That somehow does not even compare to the other 23 hours and 55 minutes when he did other things. When you exercise mutual respect you spend time listening and really considering what your partner is saying. If you don't, then you aren't showing much respect at all.

Oftentimes, we have found that couples have lost touch with what it means to communicate and spend time together. Oh, yes, they're very familiar with the concept of quality time. After all, the phrase *quality time* has become very popular in everything from secular pop psychology books to sermons from the pulpit. But they've lost touch with the concept of quality and quantity together.

Just because they spent four hours together watching two movies back to back does not mean they spent any time together. Watching television together simply does not count. When you do that, you aren't spending time together, you are spending the evening with the television!

So, true communication, true listening and loving requires quality of time and quantity of time, and mutual respect.

Often people approach communication with a conviction to be full of truthfulness. They think truthfulness is the best policy. We agree, and we don't advocate lying. However, sometimes a little diplomacy mixed in with the truthfulness would be a great benefit in any marriage. You know what we're talking about. Anyone can say something that is true and be cruel, and, on the other hand, anyone can say the same thing and be tactful.

This same principle applies to airing all of your feelings. For example, you may feel angry, but it's not going to be positive or constructive to criticize your partner or to vent your anger every time the opportunity arises. We ought not have pride in the clichés of life such as, "Well, I always tell it like it is." Well, you may, and if you do that's why you don't have any friends this side of heaven!

We need to temper ourselves, temper our feelings and consider the other person. That's why we call it listening and loving. When you listen and love, you are not only trying to communicate a message, but you are demonstrating that you care about the other person with whom you are speaking.

Then, if there is something truthful that needs to be spoken, you can temper it with the wisdom of God and words of discretion. Proverbs 2:11 NIV says, **Discretion will protect you, and understanding will guard you.**

We need to keep in mind that what we say will affect the person we are speaking to. How is it going to make our spouse feel? How will he or she respond and react?

We should make our speech gracious and easy to be received. Proverbs 16:24 paints a beautiful picture of what our words should be: **Pleasant words are as an honeycomb, sweet to the soul, and health to the bones.**

The Success of Negotiating Disagreements

In any marriage, disagreements are inevitable. It's part of life and two different people living together. And, while gracious speech will help you in disagreements, you need other skills as well to negotiate effectively. We have found, in the course of discovering how to successfully negotiate, three methods that can direct how the disagreement will conclude. They include capitulation, compromise and coexistence.

Capitulation can be defined as "giving in." In other words, one partner gives in to the other partner's wishes or desires. There's no compromise or give and take.

Now, this result may seem all bad, but that's not necessarily always the case. For example, when you leave church on Sunday, inevitably you get in the car only to have this conversation:

Husband: "Where do you want to go for lunch, honey?"

Wife: "Well, I don't know. Where do you want to go?"

Well, truthfully, they each have a place in mind. Whoever gives in to whom doesn't matter, but when they do, it's capitulation. One completely gives in to the other.

In a situation like this, capitulation is fine. It works well. When capitulation becomes a problem is when it involves something serious, like immorality, for example, or when the same one always expects the other to capitulate. So if you're going to use this method of negotiating you ought to take turns and keep score so that you keep things even. In other words, if one of you gave in last week, this week let it be the other one's turn.

The second method of negotiating is **compromise.** Staying with our dining-out example, suppose she wants Mexican food, but he wants Italian. So, you compromise and go out for Chinese! Or, in a similar example, she wants to go to the mountains for a vacation, and he wants to go to the desert. So, you compromise and go to the plains.

As Christians we often automatically think compromise is bad—and it *is* in your walk with God when you compromise His principles and commands. But when it comes to negotiating disagreements in your marriage or any other relationship, it's good. If you love your spouse and your spouse loves you, there's going to be some compromising going on to make decisions. You were raised in different households, with two different minds and two different sets of opinions. So to come to agreement, you will have to do some compromising.

Now, the third method of negotiating disagreements, **coexistence,** is one we strongly recommend you avoid.

Co-existence is when the two of you don't come to any kind of mutual agreement or mutual decision at all. You can't compromise, you can't capitulate, you can't give any ground at all, you're each firm in your position, so you just coexist. He stands his ground on his side of the decision, and she stands her ground on her side. There's no give-and-take, no coming together. And the reason this is bad is that it can sometimes result in distance coming between the two of them regarding a certain issue or area in their marriage.

Coexistence does not have to be fatal to a marriage if it involves an area that is not critical or even important. For example, going back to our dining-out example. She loves Indian food, the kind that's full of curry, and he does not *at all.* So in this situation,

It may seem like an unimportant example, but when Gene and I first got married we found we had a difference of opinion on the best ketchup and mayonnaise to buy. So we compromised and bought Gene's favorite ketchup—Heinz—and my favorite mayonnaise—Hellman's. So in this regard we both capitulated and we both compromised.

Now this may seem silly, but most major arguments in marriage are not really over important things, but silly things. So Gene and I learned early on to compromise and also, from time to time, to capitulate to each other, especially in the unimportant things. Song of Solomon 2:15 says it's "....the little foxes that spoil the vines...." So it can be the little things that can destroy a marriage or any other relationship.

—Sue

there's no capitulation, no compromise, but there is coexistence. He simply won't eat it. So if she wants it, she has to go by herself, or he may go and not eat. That's just the way it is, and that is coexistence. But in this unimportant area, coexistence is not all that important.

But consider an area of marriage that is much more critical. Consider couples who marry and they're each very tied to their own denomination and local church. She attends her church, and he attends his church. They're both Christians. She's from an evangelical church; he's from a Pentecostal church. They're in a stalemate of coexistence, and it's not good. They can't really grow together spiritually in the same way they could if they were worshiping together in the same place. In this more critical area of marriage, coexistence can be fatal to the relationship.

Coexistence is dangerous in the important areas of our marriage relationships, because to have successful marriages, we've got to be growing together, maturing together, and building one another up. So if the issue is Indian food, you'll survive the coexistence, but if it's something more serious, you really need to seek a compromise or capitulation.

What To Do With Your Anger in the Disagreements

While working through disagreements and coming to the place of capitulation, compromise or coexistence, anger is often going to be manifested in one or both partners. This is a natural response based on the fact that we come from different backgrounds. But the key factor we have to be careful about is that we do not allow anger to prevent us from effectively negotiating our disagreements.

We've all done this, however, at one time or another. Whether you're married or planning to be, anger is the point we've reached when we've stopped listening, stopped loving, stopped communicating and started arguing. And when you're arguing, there's not any capitulation; there's not any compromise; there's not any coming together whatsoever.

Anger actually stops the communicating and sharing cold, because anger is a strong emotion. And as human beings, we deal with it in one of two ways: We either suppress it or vent it, and venting it is usually destructive.

Venting anger is destructive whether you do it with words that you are sorry for later, or if you do it with behavior, such as throwing things or having a temper tantrum. Venting in either way is negative because, as we said earlier, for communication to occur, the message you send has to be received, and when you vent your anger, what you usually get back is another reaction that's usually equally as negative as the one you gave out. There is no receiving of any message you might have been trying to communicate. You're just going to get anger back.

So, the whole process of venting anger out and getting anger in return prevents proper communication. It prevents listening, and then loving can't find a place in the relationship anywhere. What we need to do is to learn how we can deal with our anger—not vent or suppress it.

Now, suppressing anger is just as destructive as venting it. If you bottle it up and keep bottling it up, even doctors will tell you the harm it can cause your physical body. At some point, if you bottle it long enough, you're going to blow the cork off, and then explode everywhere.

So how do you deal with it? You *express* it. You acknowledge it. Something we've found that works well is to just say it. Just say with your mouth and acknowledge, "Well, that makes me angry." It's amazing how effective this really is. When you acknowledge it verbally, you no longer have this need to vent it. Then you need to explain why you're angry. We know this sounds so simple, but by acknowledging your anger verbally, then explaining it, you're giving yourself the opportunity to continue in conversation and to deal with what made you angry in the first place. Then you are making positive steps toward working out the problem.

If you work out the problem, then the anger goes away. The Word says in Ephesians 4:26, **Be ye angry, and sin not: let not the sun go down upon your wrath.** According to this verse you can be angry and sin not, and, of course, you can be angry and sin. Consider this illustration: It's like standing on a street corner, getting ready to cross the street. You look to the left and then to the right. Suddenly a semi-truck blows its air horn and it's sitting 5 feet from where you're standing. In a moment of time, fear comes to your heart. Even though you are out of harm's way, it just comes. That's how emotions are. They just come. But that's not the problem, and guess what, that's not the sin. The sin is when we yield to the emotion (such as anger) or we entertain it and we give in to it. Feeling the anger isn't the sin, but venting our anger on our loved ones is the sin.

In a marriage relationship where two different, and very unique, individuals have come together, there are going to be times of being angry at one another. But oftentimes, we're angry because we don't have all the facts. And we're too angry to listen or receive, and we won't stop speaking, so we can't get the facts anyway.

The funny thing is, and you and your husband or wife have probably done this, when you later find out all the facts, you have to laugh at yourself because you were so angry for no reason! It was a useless waste of emotional energy. It was a total waste of time and energy.

So, anger is going to happen. We're created in the image of God (Genesis 1) and God Himself gets angry, but He never sins, so therefore, we can get angry and not sin as well. For example, there are numerous verses in the Bible telling of God's anger, such as Psalm 103:8-9, **The LORD is merciful and gracious, slow to anger, and plenteous in mercy. He will not always chide: neither will he keep his anger for ever.**

Even Jesus grew angry at situations: **And when he had looked round about on them with anger, being grieved for the hardness of their hearts, he saith unto the man, Stretch forth thine hand. And he stretched it out: and his hand was restored whole as the other** (Mark 3:5). But the Word also says, He never sinned: **For he hath made him to be sin for us, who knew no sin; that we might be made the righteousness of God in him** (2 Corinthians 5:21).

The apostle Paul told us in Ephesians 4:26 to be angry and sin not, and he also told us in the second half of that verse to **let not the sun go down upon your wrath.** That's why it's important, if you haven't dealt with it during the day, to definitely deal with your anger before you and your spouse turn out the lights. How many times have you gone to bed angry at your spouse, only to hug your side of the bed while he or she hugs the other side? You're lying there on your sides, backs toward one another, and it's like this great big gulf is between you. You can feel the icicles like a deep freeze down the middle of the bed. It even feels cold and nasty when you wake up in the morning. That's not the way God intended for us to live. He instructed us to be angry and sin not, and He never tells us to do something we can't do. So becoming angry and sinning not is very possible for us in our marriages if we will deal with our anger in a positive way and not yield to it.

Options in Conflict Resolution

We've talked about methods of negotiating disagreements and dealing with your anger. But in our day-to-day living there are all those conflicts that come up. Any two people who get married, work together and live in the same house are going to have conflicts. What they need in order to have a successful relationship is to learn how to resolve those conflicts. What we have found are 3 basic ways all conflicts are resolved.

The first one is **domination.** In previous chapters we've talked about the man being the head of the home, and because of a misunderstanding or misinterpretation of Ephesians 5, a lot of men think they're supposed to dominate their wives. Men, who are generally bigger and stronger than their wives, seem to think their physical statures give them the right to dominate their wives all the time. So, while we don't recommend this option, this is one way conflict can be resolved.

The second way we've found is **resolution.** This is simply the act of getting the problem resolved, of working it out, of negotiating and coming together to an agreement. This is a good option.

The third way we have found is **alienation.** This is like the coexistence we've already explained in negotiating disagreements. It results in distance and alienates one person from the other. It destroys growth toward closeness, oneness and unity.

Ideas for Negotiating Disagreements and Resolving Conflicts

While we've explained these two concepts in depth and given you methods of resolution, we also want to give you a list of ideas–actually "Do's" and "Don'ts"–to help you as you develop these skills and put them into practice.

Don't

1. Use the silent treatment. This is where you go for days on end without speaking to your husband or wife. Husbands especially love to use the silent treatment, for some reason. Instead of talking, they'll often grunt! That means they'll speak, but they never string together more than two or three words to make a complete sentence.

2. Throw your emotions at your spouse. Both men and women can do this. Women, however, usually issue a barrage of tears. But don't do it–it doesn't help.

3. Be critical or manipulative. Don't bring all kinds of pressure to bear just because you want your way. It's not right and it's going to be destructive.

4. Kitchen sink. This is when you use words such as "never" and "always." These words are hardly ever true in a conversation. It's impossible to *always* do something. When you use words like this, it's like gathering up all of your complaints in the kitchen sink and throwing them at your partner. And that doesn't lead to compromise.

5. Bring up past failures.

Do

1. Act quickly to resolve the conflict.

2. Be polite and practice common courtesy. This also means practicing your manners. Stop saying all those things that just devastate one another. Be polite to the person you love the most!

3. Stay on the subject.

4. Listen as much as you talk. There's a phrase that says, "That's why God gave us two ears and one mouth–so we would listen twice as much as we talk." Remember, when your mouth is moving, you aren't listening.

5. Seek to compromise. Come to an agreement.

Effective or Ineffective?

In addition to these do's and don'ts, use the following chart to help identify if your present methods of communicating are effective or ineffective. Use these ideas to discover other communication methods you may or may not be practicing, that you need to drop from your conversation or add to your conflict resolution skills.

Effective	Ineffective
Listening	Anger
Forgiveness	Grudge-Bearing
Sensitivity	Speaking Put-downs
Honesty	Silent Treatment
Diplomacy	Insults
Care and Concern	Profanity
Dialogue	Monologue
Calmness	Bitterness

Truthfulness	Complaining
Tact	Character Assassination
Compromise	Kitchen Sinking
	Discouraging Words
	Innuendos
	Jesting

What You Can ALWAYS Do

While you may still be evaluating what your present skills are and practicing to improve them, there are 4 basic steps to positive and effective communication that you can always do—regardless of the conversation.

First, you can walk in forgiveness. Colossians 3:13 NIV says, **Bear with each other and forgive whatever grievances you may have against one another. Forgive as the Lord forgave you.**

When we have disagreements, we ought to make sure that they do not escalate into conflict and unforgiveness. Without forgiveness and positive communication, listening and loving will cease. In fact, where there is unforgiveness, there is bitterness.

Also, part of walking in forgiveness is learning the difference between apologizing and asking for forgiveness. If I apologize, I say, "I'm sorry." That does not demand a response from you. But when I say, "I was wrong when I did thus and so. Will you forgive me?" it demands a response on your part.

In our early days of marriage, we both maneuvered our way around asking for forgiveness. We'd say, "Well, I'm sorry you feel that way." What on earth does a statement

YOU, ME AND GOD

like that mean? Nothing, absolutely nothing. It sounded like we were slighting one another, like we were saying, "You ought to be more grown up than that. You ought to be more mature than that." Saying, "Well, I'm sorry you feel that way," didn't acknowledge any wrongdoing. When we said that to each other, we were just spinning our wheels. We weren't making progress in our marriage relationship.

But when we learned to ask for forgiveness, we learned to acknowledge wrongdoing, and our asking demanded a response.

We've already quoted Colossians 3:13, but verses 12-21 NIV is a beautiful passage on forgiveness:

> Therefore, as God's chosen people, holy and dearly loved, clothe yourselves with compassion, kindness, humility, gentleness and patience.
>
> Bear with each other and forgive whatever grievances you may have against one another. Forgive as the Lord forgave you. And over all these virtues put on love, which binds them all together in perfect unity.
>
> Let the peace of Christ rule in your hearts, since as members of one body you were called to peace. And be thankful.
>
> Let the word of Christ dwell in you richly as you teach and admonish one another with all wisdom, and as you sing psalms, hymns and spiritual songs with gratitude in your hearts to God.
>
> And whatever you do, whether in word or deed, do it all in the name of the Lord Jesus, giving thanks to God the Father through him.

- 106 -

Wives, submit to your husbands, as is fitting in the Lord.

Husbands, love your wives and do not be harsh with them.

Children, obey your parents in everything, for this pleases the Lord.

Fathers, do not embitter your children, or they will become discouraged.

The second action you can always take is to walk in love. Verse 14 in the above passage says to put on love. In your conflict resolution, you have to speak the truth in love (Ephesians 4:15). You have to speak with diplomacy and courtesy. If you don't, you'll soon drive a wedge between you and your spouse. First Corinthians 16:14 TLB admonishes us saying, **And whatever you do, do it with kindness and love.**

You see, love must be outwardly expressed. Your love for your spouse is expressed by what you say and by what you do. It is communicated both verbally and nonverbally. That's how we deal with one another in other communication, and that's how we have to express our love.

Third, you can bring God into the relationship. Philippians 4:4-5 NIV says, **Rejoice in the Lord always. I will say it again: Rejoice! Let your gentleness be evident to all. The Lord is near.**

We need to bring God into our conversations and into our disagreements. As we communicate with God, it becomes the glue that holds us together. The oneness a husband and wife has is spiritual. Therefore, by speaking with God in prayer, we become more unified.

There have been times in our marriage when we simply decided that the ultimate authority in our lives, in our marriage and in a given situation, was going to be the Word of God and our relationship to Him. We decided that no disagreement, no argument, no issue was more important than unity and oneness in God. What we found was that being in agreement with God, going to Him in prayer and opening up our hearts to Him somehow just melted the problem away. What was such a big issue to each of us suddenly grew small. When you get God involved, things get resolved and come into a right perspective.

Fourth, be willing to share. This is simply being willing to come together and talk it out. You have to be willing to come to the table and work out your differences. It's so sad when either a husband or wife will contact us for help in negotiating or coming to a compromise in their marriage, and the other partner won't even come talk. The bottom line is, you can't work anything out if you aren't willing to share.

While there are many skills designed to increase the success of your communication in marriage—and we've covered many in this chapter—nothing is more important than the foundational edge God has placed in all of us as individuals and as married couples: the gift of love—the gift of Himself, for God is love (1 John 4:8,16). It is out of this love that couples can overcome anything and work out any problem. It is out of this love that couples can perfect listening and loving, *the* keys to communicating successfully day in and day out.

CHAPTER 6

Putting in What You Want to Get Out

As you learn to perfect listening and loving in your relationship, you will be practicing one of the most rewarding principles in God's Word. You will be sowing good seed into your relationship; thus, you will reap a bountiful and good harvest. That means as you sow love, unconditional acceptance, understanding, kindness and so on, you will receive those things in return.

The apostle Paul said in Galatians 6:7, **Be not deceived; God is not mocked: for whatsoever a man soweth, that shall he also reap.**

Simply put, what you put into your marriage—or any relationship—is what you will get out of it. By sowing into your relationship what you want to get out of it, you can really achieve a marriage that is like heaven on earth.

We mentioned this earlier, but in this chapter we'll dig a little deeper into this subject: Despite what the world or the magazine at the checkout stand says, it is *your* responsibility to get what you want out of your marriage. Luke 6:37-38 tells us how: **Do not judge, and you will not be judged. Do not condemn, and you will not be condemned. Forgive, and you will be forgiven. Give, and it will be given to you. A good measure, pressed down, shaken together and running over, will be poured into your lap. For with the measure you use, it will be measured to you.**

Most people use this verse in reference to money, and many churches use it at the offering time, but it doesn't mention money. The principle of giving and receiving in this verse can legitimately be applied to the subject of money, but it is not limited to money alone. This verse is a principle for life in general.

For example, if you give joy, you will receive joy. If you give meanness, you will receive meanness. If you give money, money will come back to you. So it is a principle of life—one we would do well to apply to our marriages.

So What Do You Want?

The question you need to ask yourself—and you need to answer yourself honestly—is this: "What do I want out of life?" We have discovered in our seminars and through teaching people that a lot of people want to avoid reaping what they've sown. They also want to reap where they have not sown. But neither of those are options according to God's principle of giving and receiving. Regardless of what you desire, you will reap what you've sown, and you won't reap anything other than what you've sown.

Taking this question a step further, what you also need to ask yourself is, "What do I want out of my marriage?" It might be surprising to realize that what you say you want may not be what you are sowing. It would be very interesting if someone could bug your house, install hidden cameras and record for you and your spouse what you say and do to one another. What would the results be? It might not be a bad idea to try this experiment on yourselves! So many times our ideas of what we are doing aren't truly reality, but rather what we *perceive* we are doing. All too often what we say we want out of life or our marriages just isn't what we are putting into them.

We all have expectations in life, and our happiness in life is generally related to whether or not our expectations are being met. If our expectations are reasonable, then we must understand that happiness is a by-product of successful living. You cannot manufacture happiness. Happiness is the result of being the right person—the result of you being right, doing right, thinking right, saying right and deciding to be happy. It is your responsibility—no one else's.

If you decide one day you are not happy, and you choose to go find someone else who you think can make you happy, guess what will happen after a little while? They'll stop making you happy. They'll do little things you don't like. They'll demand some things you don't want to give, and they won't make you happy! And then you'll be back on the search again. You cannot attain happiness by finding a new person to make you happy. Happiness must start by you being happy and by being right and doing right.

Often people get all burdened down with bills, the work of making a living, the commitment to all of it, and they begin to flirt around in their minds with the idea of a carefree life and running off and doing your own thing. But guess

I remember an event that occurred just after Sue and I got married. I grew up in a home you would not call a loving and nurturing environment. So basically, I really didn't know how to act in a marriage even though I loved Sue. So one of those early days I got mad about something, and for the life of me I can't remember what it was. But I really tore into Sue verbally. So here was this beautiful, petite, brand new bride shaking and trembling at the verbal abuse I was hurling her way. And you know what she said? She said, "You're just like your father!" Now don't tell me it takes weeks and months and years to change, because I know better. Even though I didn't know how to be a husband, I at least knew what I didn't want to emulate. So in a moment, I simply chose to change. And from 1976 until this day, I have never behaved like that toward my wife again.

—Gene

what? Running off and doing their own thing eventually has to lead to living somewhere. And when you get there you have to pay the electric bill and the water bill. And you have to work. And if you marry someone else and have children in that marriage, you will have crying in the night, diapers to change, teething to go through and so on. You simply cannot escape the responsibilities of life. But you can escape a miserable life and a miserable marriage. You can turn to God and His Word and His principles for success—starting with sowing what you want to reap.

So if you want to be truly happy in your marriage, sowing the right things is an important place to start. You can demand this or demand that, but it won't make anything in your relationship any better. In fact, if you've been married any length of time, you've probably already tried making demands and found the success rate to be zero. So, now is a good time to start practicing Luke 6:37-38, and begin giving what you want to get out of your relationship.

If you want her to speak peaceably to you, then speak peaceably to her. If you want him to show respect for you, then show respect to him. If you want her to lose weight, then start by taking a look at yourself in the mirror.

Your happiness is greatly affected by your expectations. That's why it is so important for your expectations to be reasonable and positive. That means they should be realistic and they should be fair. It's so important for couples to use effective communication–listening and loving–to discuss their positive expectations. Just like mutual need fulfillment, if you don't know what is important to your spouse, if you don't know what their expectations are, how can you possibly meet those expectations?

For example, one of a woman's goals probably should not be "I want my husband to be President of the United States by next year." That isn't realistic or fair. What is fair, for example, is for a woman to want a home, or to have a new dress or her own spending money every week.

Now, the husband may not think these are important, but he probably has his own expectations of the marriage that she doesn't think are important. But what you both have to do, just like you did with the concept of mutual needs fulfillment, is to respect each other and each other's expectations. You have to decide that his or her expectations are important. You have to decide that "what is important to her is important to me," or "what is important to him is important to me." If it's important to your partner, it has got to be important to you. Therefore you get in agreement, and you work on it together.

Now, this will all take a meeting of the minds. As we've reminded you several times, you are two different people from different households and backgrounds. People who go around looking for others who are just like themselves are spinning their wheels. That is not what marriage was created to accomplish.

Marriage is the coming together of two people to find completion, not competition. A man and woman in the marriage relationship are not competing, they are completing. They are completing a team. They are complementing one another. If there is a spirit of competition, then there is a spirit of division. God doesn't want a couple to have a desire to outdo one another, but rather to work together to achieve common goals.

In Amos 3:3 NIV, the prophet wrote, **Do two walk together unless they have agreed to do so?** Truthfully, in order for you and your spouse to walk together, to make your relationship a partnership, to make your marriage an ideal one, one that is like heaven on earth, you will have to agree to do it. You will have to agree to walk together and not compete, but complete one another.

In a successful marriage, you have to work together for the common good of the marriage. This means if it's good for her, then it's good for him. And if it's good for him, then it's good for her. This is because the husband and wife are one flesh.

You have to look at every situation and at every choice, together as a unit. You have to consider something's effect on the two of you as one. In other words, if something is bad for him or her, it is automatically bad for both of you. You have to judge opportunities that come your way by the value they will have on the common good of each partner. This applies to everything from your vocation to a move.

You have to ask yourselves, "Is this going to be good for us as a family?" Then you simply choose not to do those things that do not bring good to the partnership.

Start by Giving Love

If you want to change what you've been putting into your marriage and start working like a team, start with the cardinal manifestation of love–start with giving. Start by being the right person you should be in your marriage relationship. You see, love is not a passive emotion. It is something you do. It doesn't just happen. The way you get love is by giving love. And so loving someone means doing something for that person. It requires action.

Make your marriage a better one starting today. Decide what you want out of your relationship, and start putting that very thing into it. Take the words of Jesus in Luke 6:37-38 by faith:

> **Judge not, and ye shall not be judged: condemn not, and ye shall not be condemned: forgive, and ye shall be forgiven: Give, and it shall be given unto you; good measure, pressed down, and shaken together, and running over, shall men give into your bosom. For with the same measure that ye mete withal it shall be measured to you again.**

Believe them and practice them with a whole heart. When you do, God will get in it with you, and success will be yours.

Section 4

Loving for a Lifetime

Let him kiss me with the kisses of his mouth:for thy love is better than wine.

His mouth is most sweet: yea, he is altogether lovely. This is my beloved, and this is my friend.
Song of Solomon 1:2;5:16

CHAPTER 7

How to Get All the Romance You Want!

From the time we are children we are taught and trained to believe that some day when we grow up, we're going to fall in love. We're taught that the experience of it will be grand and wonderful. We're taught that love is romance, and we grow up believing all the romance novels, the concept of big hoop dresses, flowers in the fields, fainting spells, knights in shining armor—well, you get the picture. Actually, you probably remember it all too well!

Then, all of sudden, we are grown, we get married and find ourselves a few years later down the road of married life. One day, we wake up saying to ourselves, "I don't think I feel the way I used to feel. What happened? Am I even in love anymore?"

Suddenly we feel rocked in the foundation of our souls. Oftentimes we'll go to a Christian friend, counselor or a pastor. Their advice is "just stick it out." It seems to be the

"Christian" thing to do. But real marriages need real answers—and sticking it out isn't the complete answer.

We live in a society that swamps us with images of "romantic love." It's in books, magazines, on television—literally, everywhere. So it's hard to "stick it out" when your soul is crying out for romance.

Well, we have some good news—you don't have to just stick it out. You can have the romance. You can have your cake and eat it too!

In Proverbs 21:21 NIV, Solomon wrote, **He who pursues righteousness and love finds life, prosperity and honor.**

This verse holds the key to finding a true and lasting love for a lifetime. It says we are to pursue righteousness to get love, and it says we have to also pursue love itself.

If you've spent any time at all in evangelical churches, you've heard teaching on pursuing righteousness, but probably what you haven't heard enough of is the concept of pursuing love.

When you pursue love in a marriage, you pursue—yes, you guessed it—romance. You have to pursue romance in the marriage just as you pursued it when you were dating. If you don't, you may wake up one day and not only realize you feel differently than you once did, but that you're also flirting with the idea of pursuing romance outside of your marriage.

Now, this trap is just as easy for both men and women to fall into. Women, when they are thinking of having affairs, are typically seeking it for emotional reasons—reasons of the heart. When men contemplate affairs, they are typically going after the physical, after what they've seen with their eyes.

So, what women need to do inside the marriage is pursue the emotional relationship, and men need to pursue inside the marriage the physical relationship. You have to close that door in your heart and mind and say to yourself that you are not going to pursue romance outside of your marriage, but rather you are going to pursue it inside of your relationship.

So How Do You Do This?

We all have this idea that romance just happens. But it doesn't. For example, as pastors we often give advice to young people, and we tell them this: Don't hang out with other teens you don't think you would like to spend the rest of your life with. Don't date guys or girls that you don't think right up front are good candidates for spending the rest of your life with in marriage. Because, if you do, if you hang around with someone for enough days, go on enough dates, go out to enough dinners, it is almost inevitable, you will become attracted to them. There will develop a camaraderie, a sharing together, an interest in one another.

On the other hand, getting back to our marriages, if you do the opposite of what I just described and don't spend enough time together, you won't be able to keep that fire of romance burning.

We've often heard a husband or wife say something like this: "Well, I think the element of romance has been killed or has died off in my marriage." If you feel that way, then you need to understand this: Romance can be killed in any marriage, but it isn't marriage that kills the romance.

Rather, what happens is that by not pursuing romance in our marriages, we become bored with the mundane

> I remember when I first asked Sue to go out with me in high school. When she said "no" the first time, it did not dissuade me in the least. That was just part of the hunt. And she knew it. I'm sure that's why she said "no" the first time. She just did that to heighten the stakes, to make my adrenaline flow at a fuller force!
>
> I remember one day driving home and seeing little Sue Martin riding her bicycle down near where I lived. I said to myself, "Aha!" I realized rather quickly that we did not have a one-way hunt going on here. She really was interested! I knew then that whatever it took, I would win the hunt...and I did.
>
> —Gene
>
>

routine of life, and that boredom is what makes it seem as though the romance has died.

You see, that was what was so exciting about the dating relationship. It was full of surprises, and it was always fresh. When you went to pick her up for a date, you didn't know what she would have on. (Of course, she looked beautiful in everything anyway!) And she didn't know if you'd bring her flowers. The suspense alone kept her beside herself. And she never knew where you were going to take her. But she knew it would be somewhere fun and nice. All of that was always full of excitement. There was a level of interest that made the romance so exhilarating, so fun.

Well, you can have the exact same thing in marriage.

When you have two people dating, you have a man and a woman who are automatically meeting the emotional needs of one another. And the reason they are meeting the emotional needs of one another is because they are *pursuing* one another! That's what romance is! Romance is pursuit. It is the fun and exhilaration of the chase!

When people date, it's all fun and no responsibility. Generally speaking, if you're dating and still in school, there's no mortgage, there's no electric bill, no water bill. Why, if you're like so many blessed kids today, there's no car payment! So guess what? Life is all fun. And the money you spend—why, you don't even have to make a choice between feeding the baby and buying diapers or going to the theme park. The choice is automatic.

So in this situation, you have two people whose only focus in life is one another. Let's face it. We've all been there in some fashion. Even if you were in your early twenties, you acted in the way I've described. You probably started dating someone and your grades went down or your focus on the job went out the window. Why? Because you were focused on the new person in your life—not school or work. You were "in pursuit." You were "in the hunt."

Whether you realize it or not, all the way through marriage you are supposed to fan the flame, not just when you are dating. You are supposed to throw more fuel on the fire. You're supposed to get that fire roaring and keep it going. Go to nice restaurants, go to nice places, do exciting things together. When you do these kinds of things you are automatically "in the hunt" or in the game, and then you are optimally meeting the emotional needs of the other person.

When you bring into the marriage exactly what you did in the premarital chase, you avoid the death of romance.

Think about it this way. What do people do who pursue extramarital affairs? They bring into that relationship all the elements of courtship. They call one another on the phone, say sweet-nothings to one another, or meet one another for lunch. What are they doing? Pursuing romance. So why bring all the heartache of adultery into your marriage when you can pursue that romance inside your marriage?

You need to bring the excitement of the dating relationship into your marriage and keep that flame burning. You need to do what lovers do. You need to do those things that stimulate romance.

> *You know, I'm the pastor of a church. And all my life I've noticed something very, very funny about men. You can see a guy for years as Mr. Boring, Mr. Fuddy Duddy, Mr. Potbelly or Mr. Unexciting. But you get him involved in an extramarital affair and he turns into Mr. Disco King! Well, why can't he avoid all that and just move a little bit around the house with his wife? That would elicit romance!*
>
> *—Gene*
>
>

Too often men, who really achieve much of their satisfaction from their work, think, *Well, I've got the home base covered—I've got my sweetie—so now I can concentrate on my work. Why do I want to mess with all that romance stuff? That's nonsense. We're married.*

But see, that's exactly why you need to do it. You need to bring into the marriage what people do outside the marriage so that you don't lose interest in one another and wake up one day wondering to whom you are married. Twenty, 30, 40 or 50 years can pass so quickly, and you can realize all of a sudden that you're living with a stranger.

Every man especially needs to realize that once marriage is consummated, then you enroll in real life. You get an apartment and all the bills. But man is a predator. Sure he hunted the woman, and now he's got her. But he's still a predator. So it's his nature to go hunt for something else. Generally what men do is turn that attention to the job, and there's nothing wrong with that—when a man's working, he's most likely going to stay out of trouble. It's all right for a man to turn his hunting skills to money and the job, because it is his duty to provide for his home. And remember, too, that God called man and woman to rule and to multiply. So it is normal for a man to pursue dominion and success in this life through his work.

But the problem that arises is what the wife is experiencing. See, she has become accustomed to being romanced. She is used to car doors being opened for her and being taken to nice restaurants. She has gotten to where she expects to have a good time and to get lots of attention.

Well, the next thing she knows, she's slaving over a washing machine, washing dirty underwear. She's changing dirty diapers and washing dishes. She liked being taken out to eat, and now she's not only the waitress; she's also the cook! She's actually the bus person too since she probably clears the table as well. She's doing it all, and he's probably taking her for granted.

As the predator, he won her. He got her. He's got the notch in his belt for her, so to speak, and now he's turned all of his attention to the job.

As we said, in a way, there's nothing wrong with the man turning his attention to the job. Obviously, the money has to be made. There are groceries to be bought, and everyone has to have clothes. But what we're saying is that men have to be reminded that there's more going on in a marriage than just paying the electric bill and the rent.

The point is, men, neither of you have to wake up even five years into the marriage and be facing a stranger. Even though you are married, you are still in the game! You're still to be pursuing her. You're really still in the hunt!

Enjoy Your Married Life!

Married life is intended to be enjoyed, not endured! King Solomon said in Ecclesiastes 9:9 NIV, **Enjoy life with your wife, whom you love....**

So do it. Rekindle the flames of romance in your marriage. How? The same way you did when you were dating. Spend time together. Go places. Enjoy each other's company. Make time for these things because they are critical. Make time to play. If you don't, then you will lose that element of romance, for sure.

Now, sometimes men don't like to hear all of this. The first thing they think is, *Well, all that costs money.* Consider how much the failure of your marriage will cost you. We told you in an earlier chapter that divorce is the primary cause for poverty in the United States. When you divorce and the judge tells you to sell the property in so many days, you know you aren't going to get a fair and equitable price for that house. And for most Americans, their home is their number one possession. So between dividing all the assets and paying both lawyers, you have squandered all of your money!

Get it all in perspective!

Reach for the Mature Levels of Love

We've talked so much about oneness, but it's extremely vital. We have to grow closer together in becoming one flesh, and eliciting romance in the marriage is one way to achieve that. The apostle Paul wrote in First Thessalonians 3:12 NIV, **May the Lord make your love increase and overflow for each other....**

God has given us this wonderful covenant of marriage to guard, protect and nurture us. He wants us to grow in it just like we do in our relationship with Christ and members of His Body—the Church. We don't become one flesh after just a few days of married life.

No, the process takes years of sharing ourselves emotionally, socially, mentally and psychologically. And the element of romantic love, of desiring one another, is part of this growing together in oneness.

It's so wonderful to see gray-headed couples, perhaps walking down some lane in a park, laughing and joking with one another. That is the highest stage of romance. They've gone the distance. They had staying power. They made it through puppy love, the honeymoon, newlywed love and midlife romance. They increased at every level, and they still love each other. They increased through the years in feeling, knowledge and commitment. Maybe they've been together for 40, 50 or 60 years—and they have it all. They have more commitment, more knowledge of one another, more oneness and more unity than a couple who's just been together for a year or two. Why? Because we grow more in oneness through the years.

So, if you're dissatisfied with your marriage, don't stop trying. Don't bale out. Get back into the chase inside the confines of your marriage. Stand on God's Word and fan the flame of romance. Let the warmth of the fire fill your hearts once again.

CHAPTER 8

Finding the Love
That Will Never Fail

It's essential to the life and vitality of your marriage to bring romantic love into it. It's great when we begin to cultivate that romance, and we see success. We begin to enjoy our marriage again rather than just endure it like a hardship.

But there's something else even more rewarding that we need to cultivate in our marriage, and that is the kind of love that will never fail. Over the course of the years, things change and people change, but what has to remain is the element of committed love.

The Word of God calls this kind of committed love *agape* love. *Agape* is one of the Greek words for "love" found in the New Testament. It is the love with which God loves us. It a powerful form of love–so powerful that it is everlasting and unfailing.

In Proverbs 20:6 NIV, King Solomon wrote, **Many a man claims to have unfailing love, but a faithful man who can find?**

Men, you need to always remember that your wife probably dated a lot of young men, and many of them probably claimed they loved her, but she knew the difference, and she picked you. Your wife knows what she wants and needs from you. And what she really wants—and this may be why she picked you—a faithful man.

Women want faithfulness. And faithfulness is committed love. Yes, she wants romantic love too, but there is a difference between romantic love and committed love. While romantic love is great, it won't sustain a marriage over the years. That's because romance can't stay at the same level day after day after day. It ebbs and flows. What a marriage must have, and cannot survive without, is committed love. Committed love is constant, steady and sure.

And while we say women want this, truthfully, both partners desire it and have to be committed to their mates above all else in life, and above everybody else in life. It is a commitment to wanting, and working toward, the highest good for each other.

Committed Love Versus Romantic Love

To further explain the value of committed love, we have to understand that there is a difference between being in love and loving. Now being in love is not wrong, in fact, it is essential. It is that romantic love we've been encouraging you to ignite. But loving is the committed love. It is the foundational love that is "giving" in its expression, in its very nature.

Committed, *agape* love is the God-kind of love that causes us to give sacrificially. It is unconditional love. It's the love that First Corinthians 13 talks about—the kind of love that prefers one another.

We've already hinted at this, but it is important to make it clear. The supreme example of *agape* love is the Lord Jesus Christ Himself. The Word says that even before we were born, the Lord Jesus demonstrated His great unfailing love for us in that He gave His life for us. In other words, He proved His love for us. How? By His actions. So, from His example, we know that *agape* love is an action. *Agape*, committed love is something we do. It is a giving of ourselves. It is not just being in love, it is actually the act of loving.

The Scripture says in John 15:13: **Greater love hath no man than this, that a man lay down his life for his friends.** That's what Jesus did for us. He laid down His life for every person, including you and your partner.

You know, men go by what they see, whereas women go more by their emotions—generally speaking. Because of the way men are, they fantasize and use their imaginations more in the relationship. They go by their eyeballs, and that's why we, as women, need to be willing to minister to that part of a man. We have to be willing to be creative, to buy something new and wear it just for him. We have to be willing to ask him what he imagines, what his fantasy is, and as long as it is not immoral or contrary to the Word of God, be willing to be his fantasy. We have to keep and use the element of surprise. That's why I rode my bicycle that day down the street near Gene's house, because if there is a hunt going on, you have to keep the prey in sight!

—Sue

So what we are to glean from Jesus' example is that we need to avoid getting caught up in the typical Hollywood media presentation of love and marriage, where love is moving from one encounter to another, but we need to learn the selfless love of giving of ourselves for our mates.

You know, Hollywood has painted so many pictures and messages that are lodged in our minds and in our society as a whole. And most of us have stepped into married life with all of this programming in our minds. But the love that the media has presented is immature. It has never grown up emotionally.

When we are only seeking what we can get and not what we can give, then we are acting like teenagers. Most teenagers are not developed enough emotionally to truly give selflessly. They are still developing and maturing and figuring everything out in life. Their relationships are ones in which they are trying to get out of every encounter what they can. They live by what they feel. Their love is an immature love...and an immature love cannot possibly make it through all of the pressures and the realities of life.

It's impossible. There is no way an immature love can be a love that will endure the test of time.

It's a fact of life that no matter how cool or attractive you and your spouse may think you are, the time will come when you both will be considered old and out of it. And when the two of you get there, the romantic kind of love alone won't get you anywhere. It won't be enough. Let's face it, when you put your hair on in the morning and put your teeth in before you go out to greet the public, you're going to need a whole lot more than romance to sustain you!

But committed love, which stays faithful through the good times and the bad, for better and for worse, for richer and for poorer, guarantees success.

When you determine in your heart to love with committed love, when you determine in your heart to be committed to one another, then you will increase in love and in your ability to succeed in marriage—year after year.

Really, committed love is the only guarantee in marriage. We know that personally. By choosing committed love in our marriage, we know that we will always stay together, love one another, care for one another and feel the same as we did when we dated. By choosing committed love, we have chosen a love that will never fail.

Just like Jesus' love for us is based on true love, which is *agape* love, committed love is also based on *agape* love. And true love is based in faith, and it's based in hope. You can't operate in the power of true love out of your intellect or own natural ability. You have to draw that love from the God of all love. You have to have a living, active relationship with the Lord Jesus Christ, and out of your love for Him, and His love coming into you and through you, you can love as He loves. You can love unconditionally, without reserve, wholeheartedly, committedly, unfailingly.

First Corinthians 13:13 NIV says, **And now these three remain: faith, hope and love. But the greatest of these is love.**

In any enduring relationship there have to be three ingredients at work for there to be real success. There have to be faith at work, hope at work and love at work.

It takes faith to believe for a successful marriage. There will be hard times in any relationship, so you have to have faith. You have to use your faith during those times, knowing that if you do the honorable thing, and stand on God's Word, it will work out. You have to believe God.

You have to have hope that when it doesn't look like it will ever work out, regardless of how light or serious the situation, it can work out in the power of God and His promises.

And you have to have the committed love of God, the *agape* love of God, actively working in you and through you to love unconditionally.

Good Marriages Don't Just Happen

With all that we've taught you, from all the principles and strategies, one thing should be clear: good marriages don't just happen. They take work, love and dedication. They are a process of success. Just like believers develop and grow in God and thus are transformed from glory to glory, so too, our marriages grow and increase in maturity and committed love, and thus are transformed from one level of mutual fulfillment to another, from one level of joy and satisfaction to another, from one level of love to another.

As you conclude your reading of all that we've taught, don't lay this book aside and never pick it up again. Use it as a manual. Refer back to it, and let it spark your thinking and behavior. Use it as a tool to continually work on your marriage, to keep it alive, fresh and growing day after day, month after month and year after year.

When you go through seasons in which you are flourishing, rejoice! And then later when you hit a season where you feel you are floundering, always remember that every marriage can be better. So reach for it, work at it and commit to seeing it through. Sue and I have been married since 1976, and we've never stopped applying all of the principles we have taught you. Marriage is a lifelong process of mutual fulfillment and joy, if you choose it. And if you do, God will meet you in it, and guarantee your success!

—Gene and Sue

About the Authors

It was the summer of 1973 when Gene Lingerfelt submitted to the call of God on his life in a dorm room at Miami University, Oxford, Ohio. That same summer, Gene began preaching in southern Ohio at the age of 17.

Gene and Sue attended Miami University in Oxford, Ohio for one year and then Central Bible College in Springfield, Missouri, for two years, where Gene received a B.A. degree in 1976 at the age of 20.

After marrying on August 7, 1976, Gene and Sue moved to Fort Worth, Texas, to attend seminary. Little did they know that their move was to a calling, not just to a place to attend school.

In 1978, Gene and Sue began serving on the ministerial staff of a church in Fort Worth, positions they held until 1982. While in Fort Worth, they ministered in the Christian Education Department and began a ministry to young couples with just six people. Within two years, this ministry averaged more than 90 persons (not including children) in a church with an average attendance of only 500 people. Gene and Sue also founded Meadowbrook Christian School in Fort Worth. Within the first three years, the school grew to more than 120 in attendance through the leadership of the Lingerfelts.

In 1979, Sue graduated from Texas Christian University with a B.S. in Elementary Education. In 1980, Gene graduated from Texas Christian University with a Master of Divinity, and was voted "Outstanding Young Man of America" by the Jaycees that same year. In 1982, Gene and Sue left Fort Worth for Nairobi, Kenya where they served for one year as guest lecturers at the East Africa School of Theology. Most of all, Gene loved "the bush" and preaching crusades held in remote places.

During the summer and fall of 1983, the Lingerfelts traveled together doing marriage enrichment seminars and preaching from Florida to California. It was during this time that God spoke to them to establish a regional worship center in Arlington, Texas. This word was to be confirmed through nine individuals.

On January 1, 1984, Gene and Sue Lingerfelt established that church, now called the *Cathedral of Praise*. This is a work, built not by the dreams of men but by the Rhema and power of the Lord Jesus Christ: a regional worship center, dedicated to the worship of the one true God and the spreading of the faith message.

In December of 1984, Gene graduated from Southwestern Baptist Theological Seminary with a Doctorate of Ministry. Dr. Lingerfelt is also listed in the Marquis Publications: *Who's Who in Religion, Who's Who in the Southwest, Who's Who in the United States* and *Who's Who in the World.*

Since 1984, Gene and Sue Lingerfelt have pioneered more than 60 churches in El Salvador, Zimbabwe, Mexico, Honduras, Guatemala, Nicaragua and Uganda. The *Cathedral of Praise* has also purchased land, built buildings and put roofs on churches throughout Latin America. Since 1984, Gene and Sue Lingerfelt have won more than 230,000 people to Jesus Christ through altar calls in Arlington, Texas, as well as in their foreign crusades. *Cathedral of Praise* annually gives more than $1 million into the harvest fields of God around the world.

Gene and Sue Lingerfelt have also founded *Overcoming Faith Television,* seen weekly in more than 250 communities across the United States. And at the time of this publication, the *Cathedral of Praise* has more than 2,000 members and is meeting in its 1,200 seat worship facility on I-30 at the North Fielder Road exit in Arlington, Texas.

HARRISON HOUSE
Tulsa, Oklahoma 74153

Additional copies of this book are
available from your local bookstore.

The Harrison House Vision

Proclaiming the truth and the power
Of the Gospel of Jesus Christ
With excellence;

Challenging Christians to
Live victoriously,
Grow spiritually,
Know God intimately.